Financial Success for Seniors

by Robert A. Sagar

Asset Protection for Those 60 and Better™

Published by 1st World Publishing

1100 North 4th St. Suite 131, Fairfield, Iowa 52556

tel: 641-209-5000 • fax: 641-209-3001

web: www.1stworldpublishing.com

LCCN: 2007932066

Hardcover ISBN: 978-1-4218-9804-9

Softcover ISBN: 978-1-4218-9805-6

Ebook ISBN: 978-1-4218-9806-3

Contents

Contents continued on next page.

Contents, continued

This book is dedicated to:

My mother and father,
Vivian and Charles Sagar.
I am proud to be your son
and have appreciated all of your
support and guidance
for all these years.
Thank you. I love you.

Acknowledgements

I would like to thank the following individuals. Without them, my dreams might have not become a reality.

Geralyn DiPresso Sagar, for being the most caring, energetic and unselfish person I have ever known. Thank you for being my wife!

Xavier Sagar, for our unconditional commonality we share, I adore you!

Simonne Sagar, for being so caring and generous, you are enormously beautiful!

Lucien Sagar, for your unstoppable energy and willingness to always help, you are amazing!

To the three of you—I'm proud to be your father.

Rich White, for making this dream become a reality. You are a great writer and a wonderful editor.

Carol-Ann Leve, for being so frank and believing in our vision. I will always e grateful.

To everyone at The Senior Financial Center, **Vickki Kaplan, Mavel Martinez, Ken Piteo, Geralynn Scelsi, Dina Spitale, Vincent Famulari, Ande D'Addona, Julie Nissenbaum** and **Diana Korman.**

Bob Lidz, your belief in me as well as your inspiration has been priceless.

Sal Guttadauro, who, when God was giving out personalities, got more than most—and for being forever loyal.

Richard Gould, for being so genuine and electrifying.

To **Carl DiPresso,** thank you for being a great brother-in-law and a good friend.

To **Anita and Frank DiPresso,** my late mother-in-law and father-in-law, the world is very different without you in it. Thank you for your support over the years.

To my wonderful friends, **Andrew Caracciolo, Bobby Schneider, John Ianni, Angel Gonzalez, Michael Sclafani, Brandon and Shari Falchieri,** — thanks for all the honesty. Our friendships are rich!

To **Don and Nancy Mariani** —thank you for all your thoughts and creative approaches to our developments.

To everyone at Asset Marketing Systems, including **Mike Midland, John Chisam, Matt Crisci** and **Trudy Bourque,** and especially **Rick Metcalfe,** I'm so grateful for all your support.

To our accounting firm, **Granito & Epstein,** thanks for taking us on as clients!

Barbara Comer, Esq.—thanks for always making time for me.

I also want to express my gratitude to my many coaches and mentors:

To **Jim Rohn,** your thoughts and philosophies strengthen my foundation. To **Anthony Robins,** your programs have enriched my life. To **Howard Cowan,** thanks for giving me a chance. To **Sam Olshan,** I appreciate all your help. To **Warren Rosen,** you are the epitome of a true salesman. To **Dan Sullivan,** thank you for the Strategic Coach, my life has been changed forever. And to all the authors and speakers who have touched my life in one-way or another.

To **Tom Bormes,** thank you for the great beginnings.

And to all of **our clients** who have entrusted us with their lives...

Thank You!

Chapter 1

••••••••••••••

Count Your Blessings as a Senior

As a senior, you should begin each day by counting your blessings. How? Well, you could buy the license plate shown below and hang it on your wall.

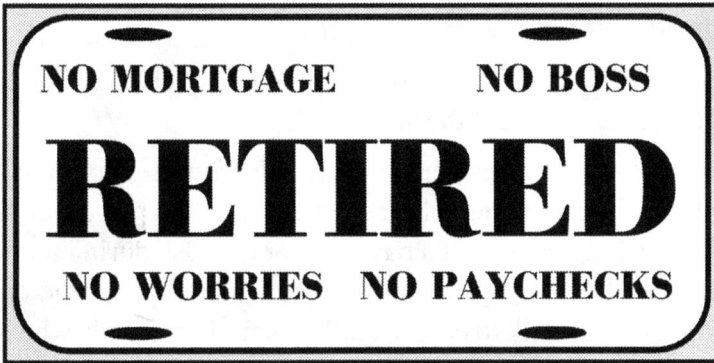

NO MORTGAGE   NO BOSS

RETIRED

NO WORRIES   NO PAYCHECKS

Is it a blessing to be retired and have "no paycheck"? You bet!

- When you don't depend on a paycheck, you don't have to worry about living "paycheck to paycheck."
- You don't need to think about how long you will stay employed and keep receiving paychecks.
- But of course, you need the confidence that your financial goals and needs can be met for the rest of your life **without a paycheck**.

Helping seniors achieve that confidence is what I do for a living, working as a Certified Senior Advisor at the firm that I founded, The Senior Financial Center. It's also my goal in writing this book.

Blessings and the Bank

Another way to count your blessings as a senior is to find a comfortable chair inside your favorite local bank and just sit there awhile, watching the world go by. If somebody from the bank staff asks what you are doing, tell them: "I'm counting my blessings."

Within a half-hour or less sitting in the bank, you would observe a few interesting things:

- The majority of customers who walk inside the bank and talk to a teller or bank officer are **seniors**.
- The majority of people who go to the ATM machine are **younger folks**.
- Most of the employees inside the bank, helping seniors get information and service, are **younger folks**.

Does this mean that seniors don't know how to use ATM machines? No, in most cases that's not the answer.

Seniors have the blessing of more leisure time, combined with a desire to do business the "old-fashioned" way — person to person. They aren't rushing to deposit a paycheck or get cash during their lunch hours, keep the boss happy or make sure the mortgage is paid on time. Seniors can afford to talk to people until they find somebody who has the knowledge they need and takes the time to understand their world.

What about those younger folks working in the bank? Personally, I have nothing against banks or youth. I myself am in my mid-40s and years younger than the clients we serve at The Senior Financial Center, all of whom are "60 and better."

But here's the reality. The financial world of most employees at your bank has more in common with the young folks in the ATM line than the seniors looking for personal help. Most bank employees are in the **asset accumulation phase** of their lives, which means saving and investing to grow more money. They have bosses, jobs and mortgages.

Your financial world is different. It includes important issues that are only vague concepts to younger folks, including Social Security benefits, pensions, annuities, Medicare and Medicaid, estate taxes and IRA distributions. You have moved through the accumulation phase of your life and reached another important phase — **asset preservation and distribution**.

Don't Become a Story

It's not just banks that don't understand your world. Most stock-brokers also live on a "different financial planet" than seniors. Their world is focused on asset accumulation, risky investments and financial transactions that generate commissions. We all have heard stories about seniors who trusted their life's savings to brokers and lost not only their principal but also their sense of financial security.

Count your blessings that you now have choices for doing personal business with financial specialists who don't work in banks or broker-age firms, but do specialize in the needs of seniors. Many of these advisors, including all of our counselors at The Senior Financial Center, have earned the Certified Senior Advisor (CSA) designation. We've "gone back to school" to learn about the special issues that seniors face in pre-serving and distributing assets, while maintaining their lifestyles with Social Security, pensions, personal savings and other income sources.

How are we different from the thousands of advisors you will find in banks, brokerage firms and other financial institutions? For one thing, I am a teacher. Since deciding to focus on the senior market in 1992, I have personally conducted hundreds of workshops among senior groups. The goal of our workshops is to impart information and ideas, so that seniors are empowered and motivated to take actions and make decisions. I tell every senior in our audiences: "I don't want you to become a story like so many you have read or heard about other seniors, with unhappy endings."

I also tell the following personal story to help seniors understand how our services at The Senior Financial Center are different...

The Whistle

From the ages of 5 through 22, I lived in Rosedale, Queens, a borough of New York City. Since most of my youth was spent in a city environment, a big treat for me was when my father would take me camping and hunting in the woods and mountains of upstate New York. Usually, these were family outings that also involved any number of our uncles and cousins. While they probably were planned months in advance, my father would never tell me we were going hunting until the night before we left.

I remember one trip when I was about 11 years old, when we went hunting in the Catskill Mountains. It was colder there than in the city. So, as was usually the case, my father had to take me into town to buy warmer clothes for the woods. Then, we went off into the woods — the older men with their shotguns and me with my little .22 — and I was assigned to stay near my cousin Artie, who was 18 years old.

About 4 o'clock that afternoon, when it began to get dark and cold, I looked up and saw Artie walking ahead… but nobody else was visible. While I tried to stay calm, Artie soon admitted that we were separated from the group and lost in the woods. As night fell over that cold and lonely mountain, I began to lose my courage and composure, just as most 11-year-olds would. After four hours lost in the dark woods, I was crying hysterically.

Then, faintly at first, I heard a familiar sound far off through the dark trees. *The whistle.* It was the same whistle my father would blow when I was lost in a department store back home. As soon as I realized that this sound was The whistle, I stopped crying. The fear and cold drained from my throat and chest and I felt safe and warm again. It took several more minutes before my father and the uncles found Artie and me. But by then we were not so scared.

For me, The whistle was a childhood symbol of safety and security. Whenever it blew, I no longer felt lost.

The Challenging Issues That Seniors Face

Today's retirees have many reasons to count their blessings every day, provided they can open their eyes in the morning and shut them at night feeling reasonable **safe and secure**.

Working with retirees exclusively since 1992, I realize that many seniors are somewhat confused and concerned about the myriad financial issues they face. At every workshop, I ask this question: "Do you think seniors face more complex issues today than ever before?" I have never had an audience answer that question "no" or even "maybe."

As a senior, you know the challenges you face. My goal is to help you meet them in a way that respects your need for safety and security, every day for the rest of your life. So, in what I am writing for you here, in what I am teaching at our workshops, and in the financial advice and service we deliver to seniors, I am trying to create for you a financial equivalent of The whistle.

Chapter 2

•••••••••••••

12 Golden Rules for Seniors

Our job at The Senior Financial Center begins with opening the minds of seniors to new ideas and solutions designed specifically for people "age 60 and better." When we first meet many seniors, most of their thinking is limited by the "traditional ideas" they have heard before — especially from banks and stock brokers. In the backs of seniors' minds, they haven't yet "crossed the bridge" from the accumulation phase to the preservation and distribution phase.

Do you have these traditional ideas buried in the back of your mind, and are they hindering you from making the best decisions? Here's a quick quiz that may help you answer those questions. Decide whether or not the five ideas below are generally true or false for seniors. Turn the page to evaluate your answers.

	<u>True</u>	<u>False</u>
1. To receive more income from my savings than the banks are paying on CDs, I need to take more risk.	____	____
2. It's not a good idea to take more money out of my IRA than the law requires, unless I need more income.	____	____
3. You don't have to worry about estate taxes unless your estate will be more than $3 million for a married couple.	____	____
4. Most seniors don't need life insurance, and they are hard to insure anyway because of age and health issues.	____	____
5. Municipal bond income is always tax-free and is the only way to receive tax-advantaged current income.	____	____

All five ideas are **false** as general rules for seniors. While they may be partly true for some people, they certainly don't apply to all. So, if you answered "true" to several of these ideas, you're reading the right book to change your thinking! Our goal is to dig out the traditional ideas buried in your mind, perhaps put there by financial advisors in your accumulation phase, and replace them with new thinking that is working great for many of today's seniors.

I've summarized these new ideas into 12 Golden Rules for Seniors, which are reviewed in this chapter and the next. Since I also cover many of these "rules" in our senior workshops, you can consider this discussion both a preview and summary of our workshop content. (If you decide to attend a workshop, you'll also get a lot more!) These rules, along with other content in this book, will help to explain why the ideas above aren't always true.

Rule #1: Don't Always Accept Traditional Thinking — Trust Your Own Experience

I tell my workshop audiences the story of the family in which the lady of the house always cut the end off the roast before putting it in the oven for Sunday dinner. When her family asked why, she said: "I don't know. It's what my Mom always did. Let's call her and find out."

They called and her mom said: "I don't know, either. It's what Grandma always did. Let's see what she says." When they asked her Grandma why she always cut the end off the roast, she said: "Because the toaster oven was two inches too short."

By the time you qualify to call yourself a "senior," you've learned many valuable lessons on your own, so you don't have to rely on "conventional wisdom." A lot has changed in recent years (like bigger ovens!). Better tools and techniques are available to today's seniors than your parents had. Some conventional wisdom, frankly, is outdated.

But your own life experience is valid, so trust it. Virtually all of the wisdom that I personally have acquired in the senior market has come from day-to-day experience working with senior clients. While they have been great teachers for me and other counselors at The Senior Financial

Center, some still don't trust their own "lifetime lessons." Recognize how much knowledge and experience you have!

Rule #2: Enjoy Your Money While You Can

Whenever my own Mom and Dad start talking about inheritances, I tell them it's not what I want. They have worked hard to accumulate money and reach the preservation phase of life. Now, I want them to have a blast!

I respect the priorities of any client who wishes to give money to younger generations or charity. But to me, there are three things in life that are more important to give away: 1) **your books**, which is a way of passing along the knowledge that you have acquired; 2) **your pictures**, which tell the story of your life; and 3) **your journals**, because a life worth living is worth recording in words and feelings.

Of course, some statistics run counter to this advice. We have now entered a period that will create the largest inter-generational transfer of wealth in history. In the U.S. alone, $13 trillion is expected to be passed down over the next 20–25 years. Even so, many seniors have false expectations about how much their inheritances may mean to their heirs. That is because today's seniors grew up in a different time, and some were born into the hardship of the Great Depression. The younger generation inheriting most of the money is Baby Boomers — the first "spendthrift" generation. According to one statistic, the average Baby Boomer will inherit $42,500 and take just 90 days to spend it.

Do you really want to live frugally your whole retirement just to make an impact on your heirs for 90 days? If you understand this reality but still want to leave money to others, then God bless you.

Rule #3: Don't Keep Long-Term Money in Short-Term Parking

The low interest rates of the past decade have helped many Americans and generally hurt seniors. If you are a young person with debts and a mortgage, low interest rates helped you qualify for credit on attractive terms and refinance mortgages at lower rates. But many seniors saw their interest on short-term CDs or money market funds decline from 6–7% in the early 1990s down to 1–2% in the 2000s.

The apparently good news during this time was that published rates of inflation also were low — and, of course, seniors are vulnerable to low inflation. But has inflation gone away? Hardly. At our workshops, I hold up a 3-cent first-class stamp and a 37-cent stamp, side by side, and tell seniors that this represents inflation during their lifetimes.

Even though the published rates of inflation have been low for a decade, it doesn't mean that the cost of living isn't higher. You pay a lot more now for stamps, cars, gas, milk, medical care, housing, utilities and many other items compared to a decade ago. You just can't earn enough interest in short-term CDs to keep pace with inflation on an after-tax basis.

Rule #4: Making Money Probably Won't Change Your Lifestyle, Losing It Will

Should seniors participate in risky investments like stocks and equity mutual funds? Of course, it depends on the individual and the risk tolerance. The "risk counseling" that investors receive when they are young, in the accumulation phase, should be different than what seniors receive in the preservation phase. At the Senior Financial Center, we believe in the "Rule of 100" for seniors. It says that if you subtract your age from 100, the remainder is the maximum percentage of your total assets that you should commit to equities. In the workshop, I also emphasize the need for caution by asking seniors two similar questions:

1. How would your lifestyle change if you invested in the stock market and your money **increased** by 30%?

2. How would your lifestyle change if you invested in the stock market and your money **decreased** by 30%?

Most seniors admit that a 30% increase would be nice, but it wouldn't necessarily change the way they live. They might take an extra vacation or two, or give more money to children or grandchildren. But day to day, their lives would continue mostly as before.

A 30% decrease, on the other hand, would probably change their lifestyles for the worse. Some amenities that seniors enjoy daily or weekly might have to be sacrificed. More importantly, seniors' sense of safety and security would be weakened. To go back to my childhood story of being lost in the woods, you would no longer hear The whistle.

Don't believe stockbrokers who tell you the odds of experiencing a 30% increase are much greater than a 30% decline in the market. That may be true over periods of 20, 30 or 40 years. But over the next few years, your golden years, the odds of large market increases and declines are about even. Why play the odds when any bad news would impact your lifestyle more than any good news?

Rule # 5: Don't Depend on Either Your Family or Medicaid for Care

As I said earlier, my childhood was spent in Rosedale, Queens. But I was born in Brooklyn, where most of my extended family lived for generations. When I was young, we would often drive back to Brooklyn to visit family on Sundays. Our first stop would usually be to visit Aunt Mary and Uncle Tommy, who owned a candy store. Upstairs lived another relative. My Uncle Tony lived around the corner and another uncle, Jimmy, lived a few miles away.

How many families today have that many people living in the same neighborhood, or even the same city? Some people think it's a blessing to have their children and grandchildren living close by — and it probably is. However, it's not a common pattern for today's families. It's probably not something you should count on when you are thinking about who will care for you if you need medical help later in life.

What about relying on Medicaid for the financial help you may need if you must go into a nursing home? The truth is that Medicaid is a "financial source of last resort" for the elderly indigent, and it should be the last choice you rely upon for care. Each state imposes "spend-down" rules that must be met to qualify for Medicaid assistance.

You can use sound financial techniques — including trusts, annuities and long-term care insurance — to maintain financial security without having to depend on either family or Medicaid for care if you get sick.

Rule #6: Bonds and Bond Funds Can Be Dangerous

Bonds or bond mutual funds are often touted (especially by brokers) as a way for seniors to earn more current income without assuming high risk. In bonds and funds with longer maturities, that's not true. The market value of these investments will decline if interest rates rise. The longer the maturity, the greater your loss can be if you must sell the bond prior to maturity.

Not long ago, I met a lady who later became our client. She was 78 years old and had $25,000 invested in each of four bonds, and she asked us if she was doing the right thing. Here's what I told her: "If your bonds are earning 8% interest or more, of course you're doing the right thing. It's enough income to live comfortably and not worry." She then admitted that her bonds were only yielding between 4.25% and 4.75%. She also said that the four bond issues were to mature in 2017, 2025, 2032 and 2098. (Believe it or not, there are bonds with maturities of up to 100 years.)

I told her that she was **not** doing the right thing for a 78-year-old person. Most or all of her bonds will probably outlive her. Her heirs will inherit them and might want to sell them. Or, interest rates could go up and she would see opportunities to earn more than 4.25% to 4.75%. To make her principal liquid, she would need to "break the bond" and sell at a loss. If you must invest in bonds as a senior, stick to maturities not longer than 10 years and preferably 5–7 years. You'll have more flexibility if interest rates increase. Ideally, you should learn about other ideas discussed in this book for increasing your income without taking more risk.

Chapter 3

•••••••••••••

Golden Rules #7 through #12

Rule #7: Look Closer at the "Tax Advantages" of IRAs

One client of The Senior Financial Center came to us with an IRA worth $780,000, of which his spouse was named beneficiary. I took one look at his situation and asked him: "Are you sure you don't want to name your two children beneficiaries instead?"

He was puzzled that I would suggest taking his wife off the beneficiary form. But his wife had already gone through the Medicaid spend-down process and was confined to a nursing home. If he died, she would receive the $780,000 only temporarily and then Medicaid would get all that remained after taxes. He just hadn't seen this possibility. When he did see it, he quickly changed the beneficiary to his children.

Of course, there also can be a problem in leaving an IRA to your children, especially if they don't need current income or want to pay taxes on it. It is possible, in some cases, to "stretch" IRA distributions to a child or grandchild beneficiary, so that he/she takes the money out gradually over life expectancy. But not all IRA custodians want the responsibility of paying out distributions over perhaps 60–70 years.

We have helped many seniors convert their IRAs into assets that their heirs receive tax free (and without going through probate) within 10 days after the client's death, and without any income or estate tax obligations. We do this by using the IRA assets to purchase a combination of guaranteed annuity income for life and tax-free life insurance death benefits paid to heirs at death. We call this our "Wealth Enhancement Strategy," and you can learn more about it in Chapter 23.

Rule #8: Pay Attention to How Your Assets Are Titled

Do you know the difference between JTTEN and JTWROS? Although most people don't, most seniors should.

- **JTTEN** stands for "joint tenants, tenants in common." It means: If the owner passes away, his/her share of the property goes through the will and is transferred through probate according to its terms.

- **JTWROS** stands for "joint tenants with rights of survivorship." It means: If the owner passes away, his/her share goes to the surviving spouse (or other named owner on the account), bypassing the will.

Sometimes, seniors say: "So what? What's the difference?"

I often clip articles in our local press to share with people who attend our workshops. In reply to that question, I produce an article that appeared on the death of a Long Island lady named Bertha Kelly, indicating that on her $1.1 million total estate that passed through probate, the total charge for all administrative expenses was $270,000. Even if her heirs paid no estate tax, they received only about 75 cents on each dollar she left them. That's what I mean about "seniors becoming a story."

I also ask seniors in our workshops if they ever had a neighbor whom they disliked, maybe somebody who was always prying into other people's business. Most people have at least one neighbor like that. If that neighbor were to pass away and leave a will, you could go down to the local county courthouse and pay a fee of $1 to receive from the clerk of the probate court a public record listing all the assets that neighbor had at the time of death, passing by will. That listing would also have to show the value of any JTTEN assets held by the deceased person's spouse — since those assets usually are divided at death and half passes into probate.

The wrong initials in titling your property can send your property through probate, instead of straight to your heirs. This could cost your heirs thousands of dollars — and also give your neighbors plenty to talk about!

Rule #9: Holding Title Jointly (With Someone Other Than Your Spouse) Can Be Hazardous to Your Health

All people, regardless of age, want to have control over their own assets. But for a variety of reasons, many seniors decide (as they advance in years) to put the name of a child, grandchild or even a close friend or relative on specific assets, up to and including their own homes. A similar habit is to put cash, jewelry or bearer securities in a safety deposit box and give a key to another person.

I've learned that many do this for one or more of three reasons: 1) They fear that their assets will be seized if they pass on or become incapacitated; 2) They don't want to have to spend the assets down to qualify for Medicaid, if need be; and 3) They don't want the assets to pass through probate and don't know any other way.

We have worked with qualified attorneys over the years to offer our clients a better choice than joint title with a non-spouse — a Revocable Living Trust. You can change the terms of the trust or even revoke it at any time during your life, and its provisions only take effect upon your death or incapacity. The assets that you pass through the trust (at death) will not be seized. They will go to your beneficiaries according to the terms of the trust without passing through probate. These assets are subject to Medicaid spend-down rules, however. So, if Medicaid is your primary concern, you might consider having an attorney draft an irrevocable trust and title assets to it during your lifetime. As long as the trust has been in effect five years prior to the time you apply for Medicaid, assets should not be subject to spend-down. (However, proposals have been made to increase this so-called "Medicaid look-back period" from 5 to 10 years.)

Several prominent "stories" involving seniors indicate why it's not wise to title a large asset, such as your home, jointly in the name of a non-spouse. In one case, a senior woman living in a nursing home put her house in the name of her son. When the son was divorced from his wife a few years later, the judge awarded the house to the divorced wife. The senior woman's son and grandchildren lost the house that she intended to leave them as part of their inheritance. In other cases, putting assets in the names of grandchildren has caused grandchildren to lose eligibility for college financial aid.

Rule #10: Taxes Are Different for Seniors

I'm thankful that my father is still alive and relatively fit at age 70. But he can be ornery.

We have a running argument that has never been resolved about municipal bonds. He claims the interest is always tax-exempt for seniors. I say it isn't. Although I've never been able to convince him, perhaps I can persuade you.

If you are married filing a joint return and have adjusted gross income above $42,000, up to 50% of your Social Security benefit is included in your taxable income and taxed the same as your income from pensions, IRAs or work. Suppose you also receive $8,000 in "tax-exempt" income from municipal bonds. This income is included in the "test" of how much Social Security is subject to tax. When combined with your other adjusted gross income, it will mean that up to 85% of your Social Security benefit is taxable, because your "modified adjusted gross income" now exceeds $44,000.

For seniors, the tax-exempt municipal bond income isn't always tax-exempt, because of its impact on the "Social Security tax." This is not something most brokerage firms selling munis will tell you — not because they are dishonest, but because their brokers don't live in your world and may not even be aware how Social Security is taxed. There are other examples of tax issues that are of more concern to seniors than younger people, including federal estate and gift taxes, generation-skipping tax, and minimum distributions from IRAs and retirement plans.

Rule #11: Use Familiar Solutions in New Ways

By the time clients see us at age "60 and better," most think they've outgrown their need for life insurance. They usually have, based on the purpose life insurance served when they were younger — namely, protecting families against premature death But life insurance can have valuable applications in the preservation and distribution phase — especially in passing assets to heirs in ways that can be planned and supervised, with great speed and tax efficiency and without going through probate.

When I make this point in workshops, somebody usually raises a hand and asks: "How likely is it that a person of my age can qualify for life insurance?" My answer is that we can usually find a quality company that will underwrite most seniors at some rating, and the rating depends on your medical history. High blood pressure and high cholesterol are so common in seniors that they usually are not big problems. Diabetes is somewhat more serious. Yet, we have had success in underwriting some diabetics with standard issue contracts. Cancer is the most serious and may require five years of remission. However, age alone is almost never a factor. I once helped to insure an 83-year-old woman who received an "ultra-preferred" rating!

My main point is not to be biased about attractive, guaranteed solutions (like life insurance) based on the feeling that you've outgrown their benefits. Open your mind to the new needs they can help you to meet.

Rule #12: Procrastination Grows More Costly as You Get Older

Since its inception, The Senior Financial Center has sponsored hundreds of financial workshops attended by many thousands of seniors — enough to fill a modest-sized stadium. Perhaps only about 40% of all these people have followed through to receive the free personal counseling sessions that we offer. Most of the rest, I've learned, fall into two groups. One group takes the knowledge gained from the workshop and applies it in their own ways — perhaps by making decisions on their own or with the help of other financial advisors. That's fine by me. We're happy to be part of their education and success.

The second group receives the knowledge and it just stays inside their heads, bottled up. They may think about it long and hard — they just can't take the step of making decisions or putting it to work. Personally, I understand that it can be hard to take forward steps after years of hearing "traditional thinking" and limited ideas from banks, brokers and others. So, it doesn't concern me **how** seniors decide to take action, or how fast. Some will ask us: "Is it okay if I bring my son or daughter into your office and we all just sit around and talk?" Our answer is always the same. We'll do it your way, as long as you are taking steps to improve your situation and avoid becoming a story.

Chapter 4

•••••••••••••

The Basics of Estate Planning

One of the best ways to understand your need for estate planning is to read accounts of what famous people left their heirs. As you'll learn later in this chapter, it's possible to know intimate details about the estates of some celebrities because the probate process requires public court documents that anyone can inspect.

Well, one Web site has done just that, inspecting the wills and other probate documents of some of America's best-known celebrities, and here is what was found:

- Walt Disney left a public estate of $23 million, of which 30% was lost to costs and taxes.
- Marilyn Monroe's heirs lost 55% of the property she publicly left behind after her death.
- John D. Rockefeller, Sr. was a shrewd businessman during his life. But after his death, costs and taxes took 64% from his heirs.
- Elvis Presley was the king of failing to plan. His $10 million public estate was reduced by 73%. When Elvis left the building for the last time, he didn't leave much for his heirs.

Source: *Estates of Famous Americans.*

This should tell you something important — namely, even if you're very successful during your life, you can still become a colossal failure in passing assets to your heirs after death. And everyone can know it!

Fortunately, an important discipline called "estate planning" can help you avoid this legacy.

Let me offer you a quick definition of estate planning. It isn't a product. It's a **process** that focuses on two main areas.

1.**Settlement of the estate.** An estate is created at death for the purpose of settling the deceased's affairs, paying debts, distributing assets, and meeting income and estate tax obligations. The estate is managed by an executor whom each person may designate before death. Otherwise, the executor is appointed by the state. There are two basic ways estates are settled. One is called "probate," a public process supervised by a local court. Probate handles all assets that pass by will or for which there are no other instructions. The alternative is to settle affairs out of court, in private. Later in this chapter, I'll explain how.

2. **Orderly transfer of assets.** Although the estate is not formed until death, estate planning can address effective ways to transfer assets during an individual's life. These ways can help to accomplish your personal goals while reducing taxes. Of course, this planning also addresses how assets will be transferred after death.

Just in the past decade or so, I've seen estate planning change from a privilege of the wealthy elite into a mainstream financial service that can benefit almost anyone. As you will see, you don't need millions of dollars to make this process worthwhile, and it doesn't have to cost a fortune. Just about anyone who wants to pass money to children, grandchildren or charities efficiently and privately can benefit from these ideas. To understand how estate planning might help you, a good "starting point" is to answer the seven questions in the checklist at the top of the next page.

Even if you answer only three or four questions "yes" or "maybe" , I think you'll find some estate planning techniques valuable.

	Yes	Maybe	No
1. Do you want to leave behind affairs that are organized and easy to settle?	___	___	___
2. Do you want to provide for a spouse who may survive you, as well as other heirs?	___	___	___
3. Are you interested in ideas for reducing estate costs and taxes?	___	___	___
4. Do you want to protect the privacy of your own and family affairs?	___	___	___
5. Do you want to prevent delays in distributing your property and avoid family friction?	___	___	___
6. Are you interested in rewarding a favorite church or charity, either during your life or after your death?	___	___	___
7. Do you own a business and want to pass its value to your surviving spouse or heirs, without responsibilities for managing it?	___	___	___

What Is Included in an Estate?

An estate is created at the moment of death, and it includes property owned outright in the deceased person's name plus half of property owned jointly with a spouse or another person. The property typically included in an estate is in bank accounts, securities accounts, your home equity (market value less mortgage balance), and tangible property such as cars and collectibles. To address a "frequently asked question" of many seniors: "Is the content of a bank safety deposit box included in an estate?" The answer is "yes," provided the executor finds it and lawfully reports its contents. Even a sock full of cash under the mattress should be included in the estate.

The death benefit on any life insurance policies owned by the deceased are included, as are IRAs and retirement plans. The **market value** of all these are totaled to arrive at the **gross estate** that potentially can be distributed to heirs.

However, before heirs get their shares, significant costs can reduce the size of the estate, and these can include:

- Debts and mortgages
- Funeral and medical bills
- Probate expenses
- State death taxes
- Federal estate taxes
- Income taxes on some assets such as IRAs and retirement plans

Heirs stand in line **behind** all of the above to receive their shares, and without estate planning, they may get a lot less than they themselves think or the deceased person hoped. With effective estate planning, all of these costs can be anticipated, managed and reduced.

The largest among the estate's expenses can be the federal estate tax, which is a graduated tax, like the federal income tax. For a reason that I will discuss shortly, the first $1.5 million of a taxable estate is not subject to tax in 2004. For example, on a taxable estate worth $2.5 million, the first $1.5 million would not be taxed. The part between $1.5 million and $2 million would be taxed at 45%. The part above $2 million would be taxed at 48%, the highest rate that applies in 2004.

The Economic Growth and Tax Relief Reduction Act (EGTRRA), passed in 2001, created a gradual reduction in the top estate tax rate, along with other changes, and I'd caution you to consider all of these to be "temporary." Here is a brief review of those changes:

- From 2004 through 2008, the top federal estate tax rate will gradually decline from 48% to 45%.
- The Applicable Exclusion Amount shields a portion of each estate from any estate tax, and it will gradually increase from $1.5 million in 2004 to $3.5 million in 2008 per estate.
- In 2010, the estate tax will be totally repealed, but only for one year. In 2011, under the general sunset provision of EGTRRA, estate taxes are due to come back again to haunt taxpayers, as if this law had not been passed. (That's why you should consider the changes temporary.)

- In 2011, federal estate tax rates are scheduled to return to those of 2002, plus a 5% surcharge that applies to the largest estates. That means the largest estates could be taxed at up to 55% in 2011, along with a reversion to a $1 million Applicable Exclusion Amount.

The table below summarizes these changes under current law.

How The Estate Tax Will Change

Year	Top Estate Tax Rate	Unified Credit
2004	48%	$1.5 million
2005	47%	$1.5 million
2006	46%	$2 million
2007	45%	$2 million
2008	45%	$2 million
2009	45%	$3.5 million
2010	Repealed	No estate tax
2011	Sunset*	$1 million

* The 2002 top rate returns and a 5% surcharge also applies to the largest estates.

The current estate tax law creates strange possibilities. If someone dies on the last day of 2010, he/she could leave $100 million free of estate tax. But if that person died one day later, the estate could owe millions, assuming "sunset" takes place as planned.

It makes you wonder exactly what Congress had in mind. Actually, our lawmakers weren't really trying to confuse people and create more business for estate planning professionals. Congress wanted to get credit for repealing the "death tax" and didn't want to throw the federal budget out of kilter beyond 2010. So, EGTRRA was the compromise.

Unlimited Marital Deduction and Applicable Exclusion

Fortunately, EGTRRA did not affect one of the most valuable estate planning tools — the Unlimited Marital Deduction, which shelters any amount of assets passed between spouses after death, provided the recipient spouse is a U.S. citizen. If a husband dies first, then his estate may pass estate tax-free to the wife. The same is true if the wife dies first and leaves everything to the husband. If either of them pass assets to a child, grandchild, other person or non-citizen spouse, the marital deduction does not apply to those assets.

The Unlimited Marital Deduction leads to one of the most important points to remember about estate planning. Assuming that a married couple wants to pass most or all assets to the other, then the spouse who will face the greatest federal estate tax cost probably will be **the one who dies last** or the **"second to die."** For example, if the husband dies first, his assets pass estate tax-free to the wife. If she then dies unmarried two years later, she has no marital deduction to shelter her estate. Even if she remarries, the marital deduction would shelter only those assets left to her second husband, not those passing to her children.

The combination of the Unlimited Marital Deduction and Applicable Exclusion Amount can work together to shelter a fairly large amount of assets from estate taxes. For example, suppose that a husband dies with wishes in place to transfer part of his assets to his spouse and another part to his children and grandchildren.

- The Unlimited Marital Deduction shelters any amount he passes to the spouse.
- The Applicable Exclusion Amount then shelters up to $1.5 million (in 2004) transferred to others, aside from the spouse.

When a single person dies, including a widow or widower, there is no Unlimited Marital Deduction, so the Applicable Exclusion Amount becomes even more important in sheltering the estate from tax.

What Assets Are Most Vulnerable to Estate Erosion?

Some assets are more vulnerable than others to being reduced by estate taxes and other settlement costs. At the top of the list are assets owned by an unmarried person, along with assets passed to a non-spouse. As you'll see, assets that are passed directly to a surviving spouse (who is a U.S. citizen) enjoy a great form of estate tax shelter.

Assets passed by a will also can be vulnerable because they may be subject to probate cost. Wills also may be more easily challenged by family members than some other ways of passing property. Any challenges can add to costs or delays.

IRAs and retirement plans also can be expensive assets to leave behind. The heir must generally pay income tax along with any estate tax. Only a surviving spouse is allowed to defer distributions and the income tax on an IRA or retirement plan by rolling it over. (A non-spouse must distribute the full amount either no later than five years after the year of death or else over his/her life expectancy starting within one year of death.)

Finally, business assets can be expensive to leave behind, especially if there is no estate planning, because the unexpected death of an owner or manager can leave the business without leadership. Heirs may not be qualified to run the business, and it may not have enough liquid assets to buy out heirs or pay estate costs and taxes.

In a nutshell, failure to create an estate plan can be very costly. Anybody can end up like Elvis.

Fortunately, estate planning offers tools and solutions that can greatly reduce the cost, and I'll review the most valuable of these tools in the next chapter.

Chapter 5

•••••••••••••

Estate Planning Tools and Techniques

To prove to our clients that estate planning isn't as complicated as they think, I tell them that the most important tool of estate planning can be created in a few minutes with a piece of paper, a pencil and a witness.

Of course, I'm talking about an updated will. Although it's not the best idea to write out your will longhand, instead of having it professionally prepared by an attorney, a "holographic" (longhand) will is usually better than nothing at all!

It's important for every senior to have a will and a living trust, and also to review and update them periodically, because these documents serve several purposes.

- The will names the executor of the estate, the person or institution responsible for wrapping up affairs.

- If the client dies while responsible for minor children, the will specifies the choice of guardian.

- The will provides instructions for assets that pass through its terms. Not all assets pass through a will. For example, most insurance benefits and retirement plans pass directly to a named beneficiary. A living trust can provide instructions passed to it during lifetime or by will.

- Having a will avoids "intestacy," which means dying without a valid will. In case of intestacy, state law determines how assets are distributed. With a will and living trust, the client takes charge of instructions, not the state.

If privacy is an estate planning goal, a will alone doesn't achieve it. Assets passed by will go into probate court, where records are public. To achieve privacy, clients must pass assets through ways other than the will, which I will discuss.

Lifetime Gifts and the Annual Gift Tax Exclusion

Another way to keep from paying estate tax on gifts is to use the Annual Gift Tax Exclusion. Each year, an individual may give up to $11,000 of assets per person exempt from federal gift tax. Under the law, this $11,000 is scheduled to increase in the future with inflation, in $1,000 increments.

However, there is a drawback to the strategy of making lifetime gifts. Once a gift is made that qualifies for the exemption, it is irrevocable. If you give your children $11,000 per year and then run out of money later in life, you can't ask them to give the money back.

Assuming that you won't need assets during your lifetime, this exclusion can allow you to greatly reduce the size of your potential estate over time. For example, suppose a married couple has three children and six grandchildren. Each spouse could give away $11,000 per year to each child and each grandchild — a total of $99,000 each or $198,000 for both. They would remove this amount from their potential taxable estates, and also avoid income tax on the future appreciation in those assets. A systematic program of transferring money by gift can help to avoid or reduce eventual estate taxes, and it only works for people who don't need access to the assets given away.

In addition to cash, seniors also may give appreciated securities, such as stocks that are now worth more than they originally cost. In this case, such a gift avoids paying the capital gains tax on the appreciation. That tax becomes the responsibility of the gift recipient and only when the securities are eventually sold. If a gift of securities is made to a child who is in the 10% federal tax bracket, then the maximum long-term capital gain rate under current law (for federal income tax purposes) is just 5% through 2008.

Titling Assets

Another important estate planning technique involves careful titling of assets to pursue specific personal goals. This is especially important for married couples, and it also can be useful for single people. The basic choices for how assets are titled include the following:

- Put the assets in your **individual name**.
- A common way a couple holds title is **joint tenancy**. Any two people may be joint tenants. When one joint tenant dies, full title automatically passes to the other tenant and avoids probate. Half of the value of joint tenancy property is included in the estate of the deceased.
- **Tenancy in common** is a way that two or more people may own property, so that the portion owned by each is specified. That portion passes by will, trust or other conveyance to the owner's heir at death and is included in the owner's estate.
- Gifts made to minor children are titled **"for the benefit of"** (FBO) these children in custodial accounts. A custodial account must have one named adult who makes decisions on the child's behalf until the child turns majority age. Assets titled to such accounts are irrevocable transfers and generally are not included in the donor's estate.
- Assets may also be titled to a **trust, a partnership or a corporation**. If the transfer is irrevocably made to one of these entities, it generally is not included in the owner's estate at death. Why is it important to review how assets are titled? 1) To make sure both spouses' Applicable Exclusion Amounts are used; 2) To title assets so as to avoid probate; 3) To title assets so as to remove them from an individual's estate; 4) And to make sure that the will is coordinated with asset titles.

Trusts

Trusts, which are among the most valuable of estate planning tools, are widely misunderstood. Some people think of trusts as documents, while others believe they are a type of bank account.

It is more accurate to think of a trust as a container designed to hold assets and convey them to your beneficiaries. The **grantor** decides which assets to put into the container and how they will be managed and distributed. These terms are then put into a trust document prepared by a qualified attorney. The person who executes the instructions contained in the trust document is the **trustee**. The trustee may be the grantor, another person or a professional who specializes in this task.

A trust may be set up either during lifetime or upon death. If it is set up during lifetime, it is called an "inter vivos trust" or "living trust." If it is set up at death, by an instruction in the will, it is called a "testamentary trust."

Perhaps the most popular type of trust used in estate planning is the **Revocable Living Trust**. Below are the key points to remember about this tool, which is popular among many seniors because it combines economy, simplicity and flexibility.

- A Revocable Living Trust may be changed or terminated at any time that the grantor is alive. Assets may be titled to the trust at any time the grantor is alive or through the will at death. The grantor can give very specific instructions on how assets are to be managed and distributed.

- Assets held by the trust at death are distributed according to the terms of the trust and bypass probate and public disclosure, which keeps the disposition of these assets private. I said earlier that I would reveal a way to avoid having your estate become known to everybody, like those of Walt Disney, Marilyn Monroe and Elvis Presley. The Revocable Living Trust is that way.

- The grantor can "self-trustee" the trust during his/her lifetime, while naming a professional to take over at death. This creates continuity, so that assets can be managed and distributed according to the grantor's wishes.

Finally, Revocable Living Trusts may be written to maximize the Applicable Exclusion Amounts of both spouses, and this can have the benefit of reducing federal estate taxes, especially upon the death of the second spouse.

An Exclusion Shelter Trust

An Exclusion Shelter Trust is an arrangement that typically uses one or more Revocable Living Trusts to pursue specific estate planning goals, especially reducing estate taxes for the second spouse to die. Here's how it can work:

- Upon the first death of a married couple, the gross estate of the first to die is divided into two parts. One part, equal to the first Applicable Exclusion Amount, is placed into a trust that names non-spouse heirs as beneficiaries. This money will go to them according to instructions in the trust document. Since the amount matches the Applicable Exclusion Amount, no estate tax is owed. The remainder of the gross estate goes to the surviving spouse and is fully sheltered from estate tax upon the Unlimited Marital Deduction.

- Upon the death of the surviving spouse, the second Applicable Exclusion Amount is fully used. Only the amount of the second estate in excess of this amount is subject to estate tax on the second death.

In summary, the Exclusion Shelter Trust seeks to reduce estate tax upon the second death of two spouses by fully using both spouses' Applicable Exclusion Amounts. A common alternative is for each spouse to leave everything to the other. But that solution can waste the Applicable Exclusion Amount of the first spouse to die. (Note: As the Applicable Exclusion Amount gradually increases in the future to $3.5 million in 2009, so will the value of this planning technique.)

The Role of Life Insurance in Estate Planning

The role of life insurance in the estate plan is to give the surviving spouse or heirs confidence that they can pay the bills due soon after a death, including debts, estate administration costs, estate taxes and the inheritance taxes that some states impose.

It is possible to have a substantial estate and not have the liquid cash to meet these payments. This can be prevented by a three-step planning discipline, as follows:

1. Estimate the cash an estate could be expected to have on hand if the client were to die today.

2. Project the cash needed to settle all of the estate's costs, including the deceased's debts, the deceased's final federal income tax, federal estate tax and any state inheritance taxes.

3. Fill any gap between the amount in steps 1 and 2 with life insurance.

Life insurance works well to fill this gap because it can be paid quickly to the named beneficiary upon presentation of a death certificate, and it avoids probate. Life insurance also enjoys important tax advantages that make it attractive in planning for estate costs and taxes.

- The death benefit is not subject to income tax.

- During the owner's lifetime, loans from many "permanent life insurance" programs may be taken tax-free. Also, partial withdrawals of cash value may be taken tax-free, up to the basis paid into the policy.

- The death benefit is not included in the estate when the deceased does not own or control the policy — for example, by holding the insurance in an Irrevocable Life Insurance Trust (ILIT). (See Chapter 23 for more information on this technique.)

Life insurance isn't the only way to plan ahead for paying estate costs and taxes. For example, an alternative is to have the estate sell property or investments, or even borrow money. But these payment methods can be complex for estate executors to evaluate, and they may require heirs to agree on terms.

Life insurance works well to pre-fund estate costs because it can be both easy and economical. It generally makes the whole experience better for the executor and heirs, too.

Chapter 6

•••••••••••••

Advanced Estate Planning Concepts

The ideas I've covered in the two previous chapters on estate planning can work for almost any senior, whether or not you expect any estate taxes to be owed. In this chapter, I'll cover ideas that can be useful if you expect to have a large estate or somewhat complex planning needs.

Income in Respect to Decedent (IRD)

We've already discussed many types of complexities and expenses that estates can face. One of the least known (but commonly encountered) areas to consider is called Income in Respect to Decedent (IRD). It is defined in IRS Publication 559 as "all gross income that the decedent would have received had death not occurred, and that was not properly included on the final return of the deceased."

It may help to think of IRD as a "conduit." This conduit funnels income that would have been taxable to the deceased to a beneficiary. The law generally says: "If income goes through the conduit and would have been taxable to the deceased, had death not occurred, then it must be taxed anyway to the beneficiary."

For reporting purposes, IRD is reported by the decedent's estate if the estate receives it, by the beneficiary if the right to income passes directly to the beneficiary, or by any person to whom the estate gives the right to receive it. IRD creates an income tax obligation, not an estate tax obligation. In most cases, it's an obligation of the beneficiary.

Here are some common sources of IRD:

• Savings bonds

- Installment contracts receivable
- Non-qualified annuities
- Deferred compensation agreements
- Unpaid salary or wages at death
- Lump-sum distributions of retirement plan assets after death (except for post-tax contributions)

The IRD Deduction

Perhaps the most complex element involving IRD is the so-called "IRD deduction." To explain it, imagine two scenarios. In the first, the owner of an assets lives and pays income tax. In the second, the owner dies and passes the asset and IRD obligation to a beneficiary.

In the first example, the income is taxed during the owner's lifetime. At death, the owner's taxable estate is reduced by the amount of income tax paid. So, the estate tax bite is correspondingly smaller, because tax has already been taken.

In the second example, if the beneficiary received IRD after death, the taxable estate has already been determined — without regard to the IRD. So, the estate tax would be calculated on the whole amount, including income tax paid. That creates a kind of "tax windfall" for the government.

The IRD deduction eliminates this windfall. It makes available an income tax deduction to the taxpayer who receives and reports the IRD. This deduction equals the estate tax paid on the IRD that the taxpayer receives. In effect, the IRS gives back the amount of extra estate tax that it collected because death occurred. But it issues this refund as an income tax deduction, not an estate tax deduction.

Responsibilities of an Executor

Among the most important estate planning choices that a senior faces is the appointment of an executor. If I am asked for an opinion, I suggest naming as executor either your own spouse or a trusted and responsible child or relative who lives nearby. Since the executor has so many responsibilities that demand proximity to the affairs of the deceased, it's important that the executor be somewhat local. I've seen cases in which executors had to spend many hours before estates were finally settled. So, it's also important to choose an executor who is willing to devote time and energy to the job. (Note: The courts allow executors to be paid a reasonable fee for their work.)

The executor's specific legal responsibilities vary among the states. The list below contains responsibilities that are common to most states:

- Help with funeral arrangements
- Hire an attorney to handle legal matters that affect the estate
- File the will in probate court and attend probate hearings
- Notify creditors of the deceased's death
- Inventory all safe deposit boxes owned by the deceased in accordance with federal and state requirements
- Locate the deceased person's property; prepare and file an inventory of the estate's assets
- File death notification and claims with insurance companies.
- Collect and review mail sent to the deceased
- Maintain records of all income, expenses and other transactions on behalf of the estate
- Pay approved bills for which the estate is responsible.
- Notify beneficiaries of the progress of estate settlement.
- File claims for Social Security and other government benefits that are due the estate
- Distribute personal property according to the terms of the will
- Arrange for transfer of real estate title(s)
- Prepare and file a final income tax return for the deceased and required estate tax returns.
- Consider tax consequences for the beneficiaries in selecting the date to distribute the assets from the estate
- Prepare final accounting of all transactions for the estate

Members of an Estate Planning Team

For estates that are large or complex, estate planning may be conducted through a "team approach" that involves several experienced professionals. The following are some specialists that you may want to consider for your team:

- **Estate Planning Attorney** — The attorney's role includes drafting of wills, trusts and related documents, and also, in some cases, analysis of legal issues involved in estate tax, estate administration, property titles and trust administration. Look for attorneys who have a practice specialty area in estate planning.

- **Certified Public Accountant (CPA)** — The CPA's role typically is to offer advice and opinion involving income tax consequences of gifts or trusts during the donor/grantor's lifetime, and to complete tax returns, including the final income tax return of the deceased. CPAs can perform the calculations involved in required minimum distribution from retirement plans and the proper tax deduction for charitable gifts. Some CPAs also have knowledge of estate tax issues.

- **Life Underwriter** — A life insurance professional with proper credentials, such as a CLU or ChFC designation, can assist with the evaluation and selection of life insurance coverage needed to plan for estate settlement costs and taxes. The life underwriter also can help to determine policy ownership issues, such as whether to use an ILIT and selection of a beneficiary.

- **Trust Officer** — Trust officers may act as personal administrators and also as corporate trustees of trusts. Typically, a trust officer is an employee of a bank or trust company who has experience acting as a fiduciary. Employing trust officers can help to reduce friction between heirs or family members, and it also can add continuity to investment management. A professional trust officer usually is supported by a capable staff, including a successor who can take over if necessary.

- **Valuation Experts** — A valuation expert is useful in helping small business owners determine the fair market value of privately held businesses for purposes of arranging buy-sell agreements and other elements of succession planning. The valuation expert also may be useful in valuing some types of property donated to a charitable trust or gift annuity arrangement.

- **Development Officer** — A development officer is a specialist in arranging charitable gifts, perhaps for a specific institution. This professional can help donors evaluate alternative strategies for making gifts while fulfilling personal objectives.
- **Financial Planner** — A financial planner may act as a generalist on the team, helping to coordinate other professionals while adding expertise in insurance, investments and goal-setting. Many planners have earned professional designations including CFP, CLU, ChFC or the highly specialized CSA.

Glossary of Key Estate Planning Terms

Administrator	An entity appointed to oversee the estate of a deceased person who dies without a will. The administrator performs duties similar to an executor. In some states, an administrator is called a "personal representative."
Beneficiary	The person or entity designated to benefit from an asset, the estate or a trust.
Codicil	A written addition or amendment to a will.
Conservator	An individual or financial institution responsible for administering the assets or affairs of a *minor* child's or legally incapacitated person's assets or rights. The conservator acts until the child becomes a legal adult or the incapacitated person recovers. In some states, a conservator is called a "guardian of the state."
Donor	A person who makes a gift to a charity or another person. A person who sets up a trust and transfers gifts to or through it is called a "grantor/donor."
Gross Estate	All of a deceased person's property or assets that are included in the calculation of federal estate tax.

Executor   An individual or financial institution named or appointed to administer the estate of a deceased person. In some states, the executor is called a "personal representative."

Fiduciary   An individual or financial institution that acts in a position of confidence and trust on behalf of others. Executors, trustees and guardians are examples of fiduciaries.

Grantor   The person who establishes a trust.

Guardian   A competent adult who acts on behalf of a minor or legally incapacitated person, making decisions in that person's best interest.

Heir   One who inherits property from a deceased, whether it is passed by will, by trust or directly to a named beneficiary.

Irrevocable Trust   A type of trust in which the grantor gives up control over assets and may have limited power to make changes in the trust's terms.

Living Trust   A trust established while the grantor is alive, in which the grantor retains control of assets and has broad ability to make changes in trust terms. It is also called an "inter vivos trust."

Probate   A public court proceeding to validate the will of a deceased person and oversee the supervision of the deceased's assets and liabilities. A probate court judge may rule to settle disputes about the will involving family members, creditors, heirs or business partners.

Testamentary Trust A trust that is established by the will and takes effect after death.

Testator   The person who makes a will.

Trust   A written agreement that expresses the will of a grantor to provide for the transfer or management of assets.

Trustee   An individual or institution that acts to carry out the terms of a trust in accordance with the grantor's wishes and applicable law. A trust may have more than one trustee. A "successor trustee" may be named to take over on the demise of the primary trustee. A "corporate trustee" is a qualified financial institution that offers high-level professional services in supervising trusts and managing their assets.

Will   A document created by a testator to indicate wishes for transferring property at death. The will also may contain the testator's wishes for appointment of a guardian for minor children and an executor for the estate. It may designate gifts and contain funeral and burial instructions.

Chapter 7

••••••••••••••

How to Prepare for a Retirement Plan Distribution

As retirement approaches, one of the most important financial decisions that many seniors make involves the distribution of money from their retirement plans. Typically, a few months before you retire, you will be invited to visit the Human Resources office of your employer and told about your options for taking all your plan money when you leave work.

Most companies don't want the responsibility of administering retirement plan accounts for workers who have retired or gone to work elsewhere. Also, in today's economy, the trend is toward "portable pensions" that workers can take with them from job to job, so that their retirement plan money can keep growing over whole careers, perhaps across many jobs. While this can be a benefit to younger workers, it puts extra pressure on retiring people at a time when they may face many other difficult decisions.

At The Senior Financial Center, we've met with many people who don't feel prepared to make the complex tax and investment decisions required at retirement, especially involving plan money at work. I urge these people to take a deep breath, relax and not make decisions in haste. Even if Human Resources people at work are pressuring you to act, **take your time**. Learn the important facts and understand all your options before you leap at any particular plan of action. You really can't start doing this too soon, either. Once it becomes "official" that you are retiring, don't wait for the Human Resource office to call you. Take the initiative to get the information you need as soon as possible!

Six Trigger Events

In terms of learning about retirement plan distributions, a good place to start is with the concept of a "trigger event." This is an event at which your plan money can be distributed to you under federal law. The six trigger events are: 1) separation from service (e.g., quitting, being fired, being offered early retirement); 2) reaching retirement age; 3) reaching age 59½ in a plan that allows distributions after that age; 4) death; 5) disability; and 6) termination of the plan.

At a trigger event, participants normally are entitled to receive their vested plan balances, less any plan loans outstanding. For many people, this is the "biggest paycheck" they may ever handle, representing years of personal savings, employer contributions and accumulated plan earnings. Perhaps the most important point to make about handling a distribution involves the need to anticipate and plan for trigger events. For example, if your company is downsizing and laying off workers, don't wait for "pink slip day" to seek information or advice. Likewise, if you believe you may be included in an "early retirement buyout offer," start gathering information about your options right away.

One of the first steps in planning for a trigger event is to understand all your choices for handling this money, and then select the best one for your future.

Your Choices Are Many

You will probably have several of the following choices for handling this money:

- **Leave money in the plan and let it compound.** In most cases, you can't be required to take a distribution unless your plan balance is fairly small. However, leaving money in the plan means you will be limited to the plan's investment choices. Also, you may not be allowed to put more of your own money into the plan after you leave work.

- **Take an annuity income payout from the plan, if one is offered.** This choice converts plan money into a steady income that may be guaranteed by an insurance company. However, once you accept this choice, you generally can't change it. Most plans offer only a limited selection of annuity payout choices, and these may not be competitive with the "rates" (guaranteed income) you could receive if you could shop on the "open market."

- **Pay tax on the distribution and invest or spend the after-tax amounts.** This is usually not an attractive choice — especially if your biggest paycheck is large. The distribution will be added to your other income and could be taxed in the highest brackets. If you are under age 59½, the distribution also could be subject to a 10% federal tax penalty.

- **Transfer the money to the plan of a new employer, if this option is offered.** Recent tax law changes encourage transfers between companies and types of plans. To make this choice work, you generally need to have a new job lined up and take steps to make sure your money is transferred from one plan to another. In this case, you won't owe current income tax on amounts transferred and all your plan money can continue to grow. If you don't have a new job lined up, you may be able to make a plan-to-plan transfer through use of a "conduit IRA," a temporary IRA used specifically to hold plan money in between jobs.

- **You can transfer the money directly to a Traditional IRA in your own name.** You must arrange this transfer between the company you are leaving and your choice of IRA provider. In this case, you do not actually receive money and there is no current income tax consequence.

- **You can receive the distribution and then "roll it over" to a Traditional IRA in your own name.** You must deposit money into the IRA within 60 days of receipt. The employer will withhold 20% of the distribution for federal income tax, so you will have to supply this amount yourself if you want to avoid tax on 100% of your money. It's best to avoid the withholding issues of a rollover, if you can.

- **You may transfer or roll over money to a Traditional IRA and then convert to a Roth IRA, if you qualify.** Roth conversions currently are available to taxpayers with modified Adjusted Gross

Income (AGI) of $100,000 or less. In a Roth conversion, you pay current income tax on the converted amount and then can qualify for tax-free distributions later on.

Which Choice Is Best?

These choices can be complex to evaluate. With so much money at stake, you need to make sure your analysis is thorough and considers your long-term retirement planning and income needs. That's why it usually pays to sit down with a financial professional well before a trigger event. At The Senior Financial Center, we help retiring clients by showing them the projected consequences of different choices, using customized software and illustrations. We also prefer to integrate this analysis with the retirement planning process in general, including your attitudes about financial security, risk, helping children or grandchildren, and pursuing lifetime dreams such as home relocation or travel.

If you prefer a guaranteed annuity payout, for example, your choice isn't limited to the one offered by your plan. We (or another professional advisor of your choice) can help you compare income payouts and the quality of guarantees available from other insurance companies.

When you consider how long and hard you have worked to earn your biggest paycheck, you should then decide that it's worthwhile to make the most of it with qualified professional help.

Chapter 8

••••••••••••••

Required Distributions from Retirement Plans

It's not often that the IRS gives millions of seniors a gift. But for retired people who take "minimum distributions" from IRAs, that is exactly what happened a few years ago. In 2003, the IRS finalized a new table that determines the "minimum distributions" required to be taken from Traditional IRAs and company retirement plans each year after turning age 70½. Not only did seniors catch a break in terms of income taxes — but the new regulations also made the annual calculation of required minimum distributions much simpler, too. (Note: Minimum distributions are not required from Roth IRAs.)

Minimum Distributions during Your Lifetime

Here are the main points that seniors should understand about taking minimum distributions from Traditional IRAs or retirement plans during their lifetimes.

- The most important term to know is **Required Beginning Date (RBD)**. The RBD is the date on which minimum distributions must begin during the owner's lifetime, and that is the **later** of:

- April 1 of the year following the year in which the owner reaches age 70½, or,

- The year of retirement (for employees who are not 5% owners of their own companies).

- The first required distribution must be made by the RDB for the year in which the owner turns 70½ (or retires, if later). In that same year, and each following year, minimum distributions also are made by 12/31 until the owner dies or assets are depleted.

- How much money must be distributed each year? Almost everyone may now use the same "Uniform Table" shown at right.

- Each year's calculation is very simple, for most people: Divide the account balance on 12/31 of **the prior year** by the table value, determined by age. Since the table extends to age 115, it is possible to meet all requirements and still have some money left in your retirement plan until well after you turn age 100.

- Under the changed IRS regulations, the distribution amount no longer depends on the beneficiary named — unless the beneficiary is a spouse more than 10 years younger. In that case, the calculation is based upon the joint life expectancy of the account owner and spouse.

- For workplace retirement plans, a separate minimum distribution calculation may be required for each plan. However, if a senior owns several Traditional IRAs, they may be combined into one simple calculation and one annual distribution (during the client's own lifetime). This is a benefit of transferring or rolling over company plan money into Traditional IRAs. You may take the required distribution from any of your Traditional IRAs, or a combination of several.

Let's consider an example, so that you will see how the Uniform Table works. For a client age 77 who names a spouse (not more than 10 years younger) as beneficiary, the Uniform Table divisor is 21.2 years. Assume the account balance on 12/31 of the previous year was $500,000. The minimum distribution for the year, which must be taken by 12/31, is calculated by dividing $500,000 by 21.2. The result is $23,585.

Minimum Distributions after Death

Another important term to remember, for purposes of understanding minimum distribution requirements from retirement plans after death, is "designated beneficiary" (DB). This is an individual named to receive Traditional IRA or qualified plan assets at death. This individual is designated on September 30 of the year after the year in which the owner dies.

"Uniform Table" for Determining
Annual Required Minimum Distributions

Age	Divisor	Age	Divisor	Age	Divisor
70	27.4	86	14.1	102	5.5
71	26.5	87	13.4	103	5.2
72	25.6	88	12.7	104	4.9
73	24.7	89	12.0	105	4.5
74	23.8	90	11.4	106	4.2
75	22.9	91	10.8	107	3.9
76	22.0	92	10.2	108	3.7
77	21.2	93	9.6	109	3.4
78	20.3	94	9.1	110	3.1
79	19.5	95	8.6	111	2.9
80	18.7	96	8.1	112	2.6
81	17.9	97	7.6	113	2.4
82	17.1	98	7.1	114	2.1
83	16.3	99	6.7	115+	1.9
84	15.5	100	6.3		
85	14.8	101	5.9		

If the account has multiple beneficiaries, the beneficiary with the shortest life expectancy is considered the DB, assuming that all beneficiaries are individuals.

Assuming that you die holding a Traditional IRA or retirement plan before reaching RDB, the minimum distribution requirement depends on whether or not your spouse is your "sole DB." A sole spouse DB may treat the account of the deceased owner as his/her own, which is effectively the same as a transfer rollover. The owner's name comes off the plan and the sole spouse DB's name goes on. That means the spouse can defer distributions until his/her own RBD while naming new beneficiaries. **Remember:** Only a sole spouse DB enjoys this option.

Any DB (including a sole spouse) may have two other choices. The IRS calls these "Rule 1" and "Rule 2" in its Publication 590, which contains definitive explanations and instructions for minimum distributions.

- **Under Rule #1**, the entire interest must be distributed by the fifth year following the year of death. If this choice is elected, there are no minimum distribution requirements in the first four years following death. For example, suppose the account owner dies in 2005. Any DB may choose to distribute all plan money by 12/31/10. If any beneficiary is a non-individual, such as a trust or charity, Rule #1 automatically applies.

- **Under Rule #2**, the entire interest must be distributed over a period not exceeding the life expectancy of the DB, using an IRS Ordinary Life Annuity Table. The minimum distribution must begin for a spouse DB by the later of 12/31 of the year following death or 12/31 of the year in which the owner would have reached 70 ½. In other words, a spouse DB, and only a spouse DB, may delay distributions at least as long as the owner could have while alive. But for a non-spouse DB, Rule #2 always means taking the first distribution by 12/31 of the year following death.

Now, let's consider another possibility — that the owner dies on or after the RBD. In other words, the owner has turned 70½ and taken at least the first minimum distribution and then dies. In this case, for any individual DB, the same basic choices (Rule #1 and Rule #2) still apply, with one major exception: The beneficiary who receives the assets must take the owner's final distribution due in the year of death, using the same method that applied to the owner.

These are probably the most complex regulations you will encounter in this book, and I believe it can be important for seniors to understand them. The regulations generally favor naming your own spouse as your DB, unless you have a specific reason not to. One valid reason can be a desire to stretch out the required distributions (and taxes on them) as far into the future as possible. If this is your goal, you can name a child or grandchild as DB, and that person could take distributions over his/her life expectancy, which might be another 50 or more years.

Advantages of Roth Conversions

In many cases, a Roth IRA can be useful in accumulating and passing on estates.

For purposes of accumulating assets during the owner's lifetime, the owner may continue to make post-tax contributions to a Roth IRA at any age. In a Traditional IRA, contributions are not allowed after age 70½. Also, there are no required minimum distributions for Roth IRA owners during their lifetimes. In a Roth IRA, no income tax is due on qualified distributions during the owner's life or after death, after a five-year holding period has been established.

This means it can be useful for seniors to establish and fund Roth IRAs. By the year 2008, a person age 50 or older will be allowed to contribute $6,000 annually to a Roth IRA, and such contributions can continue to any age. Also, conversions of Traditional IRAs to Roth IRAs may make sense for taxpayers who qualify — single or joint filers with AGI below $100,000.

A good time to make a Roth conversion is as age 70½ approaches, since the conversion can be an instant solution to all future minimum distribution chores while allowing your contributions to continue. Since the converted amount is added to taxable income in the year of conversion, you may save taxes by converting "pieces" of a Traditional IRA to a Roth IRA over several years. This avoids having the converted amount push other taxable income into higher tax brackets.

Because the full value of a Roth IRA normally is included in the owner's estate at death, there are no estate tax advantages to Roth conversions.

Chapter 9

•••••••••••••

Planning Your Income in Retirement

Most seniors have a pretty good idea of the amount of income they would like to receive in retirement to feel financially secure while maintaining their normal lifestyles. Let's say that for a given couple about to retire, that amount is $4,500 per month.

Can they count on that much income from a combination of Social Security benefits, pensions and annuities, retirement plan payouts and personal savings/investments?

That's an important question, and it's not always the first question I'll pose — because I am not taking for granted that the $4,500 number (in their heads) is actually the right amount that should be their goal. Before I'm satisfied, I may ask them to better define three categories of retirement income: needs, wants and rewards.

- Your **needs** are the essential items and expenses that are required to support your retirement lifestyle, such as clothing, rent or mortgage payment, utilities and basic transportation.

- Your **wants** are the extras that define the quality of your retirement lifestyle. Examples include a new car, vacations or travel, entertainment and luxuries.

- Your **rewards** are special goals that will make your retirement really special and successful, such as buying a vacation home, taking a trip around the world, or leaving a legacy for charity or heirs.

Of course, anything can happen over today's long retirement periods. It's hard to know for sure how much income you will need, especially when you account for future inflation in costs. However, I believe that being as specific as you can about your needs, wants and rewards is a great way to start planning. To help you, I've developed a worksheet called *Defining Your Needs, Wants and Rewards*. I encourage you to sit down with it for a few minutes, pencil in hand, and start planning!

Use a pencil, because you'll probably find that your "first guess" number for some types of expenses is not accurate, after you get out your checkbook stubs and make sure. Also, I encourage married couples to think carefully about how their expenses may change during retirement. In this exercise, debate between spouses is healthy!

Keep in mind that the goal of this exercise is to create a budget (in three parts) during the first year of retirement. If you have already begun your retirement, then you can assume that this is the first year, for this purpose.

My best advice to seniors is that they should focus their budgeting and planning mainly on making sure that they can afford their needs and wants over their life expectancies, plus a "margin of comfort." If your life expectancy in the first year of retirement is 15–20 years, a margin of comfort might be an extra 3–5 years beyond that. Of course, you also must factor into this process a realistic rate for future inflation in costs.

Once you feel confident that your income will meet your inflation-adjusted needs and wants in retirement, you then can think about affording some luxuries. For most people, leaving money to heirs is (and should be) considered a luxury. You've worked hard a long time to reach retirement — and your own financial security and happiness should come first. But there can be valid exceptions, such as providing money for a disabled child or grandchild, or helping grandchildren pay part of their college tuitions. If these are your priorities and you want to consider them "wants" instead of "rewards," it's your choice.

As time passes and your goals change, you can always update this worksheet. You can also use it to communicate your ideas about a successful retirement to a spouse or any financial advisor(s) who may help you.

Instructions for Using the Table

1. Start with the line on the *Needs, Wants and Rewards Worksheet* that says: Total estimated monthly expenses for Needs and Wants. Multiply this number by 12 (months) and consider this a "base amount" monthly income in the first year of retirement.

2. Using *the Inflation-Adjusted Future Income Table*, select the average rate of inflation you wish to project over your retirement, from 2–8%, in the top row.

3. Find the factor for this rate for any given year of your retirement. For example, assuming a 4% rate of inflation, the factor for the 20th year of retirement is 2.19.

4. Multiply your total Needs and Wants per month in the first year of retirement by this factor to determine projected Needs and Wants in the future. For example, if your Needs and Wants are $3,500 per month in the first year of retirement, multiplying by the factor for a 4% inflation rate in the 20th year: $3,500 x 2.19 = $7,665.

5. In this example, Needs and Wants are projected at $7,665 per month in the 20th year of retirement and increase at 4% average annual inflation.

You can use the *Summary Income Worksheet* to list your projected inflation-adjusted Needs and Wants in each year of retirement. Then, use the same worksheet to project the amount of total income you can project from each of five sources:

1. Wages or self-employment income (if you keep working in retirement)

2. Social Security

3. Pensions and annuities

4. Retirement plan payouts

5. Personal savings and investments

Add these five columns (for each year) to project how much income you can expect. Ideally, these five income sources should equal at least the total of your Needs ad Wants in each year of retirement.

Needs, Wants and Rewards Worksheet

Fill in your estimated monthly expenses in the first year of retirement.

Your NEEDS: *Essentials that will support your retirement lifestyle.*

Food	$_____
Clothing	$_____
Rent or mortgage payment	$_____
Utilities	$_____
Basic transportation	$_____
Medical insurance and costs	$_____
Taxes	$_____
Other:_____	$_____
Total	**$_____**

Your WANTS: *Extras that define the qualify of your retirement lifestyle.*

New car	$_____
Vacations or travel	$_____
Nicer, newer clothes	$_____
Dining out more often	$_____
Entertaining friends and family	$_____
Pursuing hobbies and recreation	$_____
Joining clubs	$_____
Other:_____	$_____
Total	**$_____**

Your REWARDS: *Special goals that help you feel successful.*

Recreation vehicle or motor home	$_____
Legacy for heirs	$_____
Vacation home	$_____
Trip around the world	$_____
Gifts to help children or grandchildren	$_____
Other:_____	$_____
Total	**$_____**

Inflation-Adjusted Future Income Table

Year of Retirement	Projected Rate of Inflation						
	2%	**3%**	**4%**	**5%**	**6%**	**7%**	**8%**
1	1.02	1.03	1.04	1.05	1.06	1.07	1.08
2	1.04	1.06	1.08	1.10	1.12	1.14	1.17
3	1.06	1.09	1.12	1.16	1.19	1.23	1.26
4	1.08	1.13	1.17	1.22	1.26	1.31	1.36
5	1.10	1.16	1.22	1.28	1.34	1.40	1.47
6	1.13	1.19	1.27	1.34	1.42	1.50	1.59
7	1.15	1.23	1.32	1.41	1.50	1.61	1.71
8	1.17	1.27	1.37	1.48	1.59	1.72	1.85
9	1.20	1.30	1.42	1.55	1.69	1.84	2.00
10	1.22	1.34	1.48	1.63	1.79	1.97	2.16
11	1.24	1.38	1.54	1.71	1.90	2.10	2.33
12	1.27	1.43	1.60	1.80	2.01	2.25	2.52
13	1.29	1.47	1.67	1.89	2.13	2.41	2.72
14	1.32	1.51	1.73	1.98	2.26	2.58	2.94
15	1.35	1.56	1.80	2.08	2.40	2.76	3.17
16	1.37	1.60	1.87	2.18	2.54	2.95	3.43
17	1.40	1.65	1.95	2.29	2.69	3.16	3.70
18	1.43	1.70	2.03	2.41	2.85	3.38	4.00
19	1.46	1.75	2.11	2.53	3.03	3.62	4.32
20	1.49	1.81	2.19	2.65	3.21	3.87	4.66
21	1.52	1.86	2.28	2.79	3.40	4.14	5.03
22	1.55	1.92	2.37	2.93	3.60	4.43	5.44
23	1.58	1.97	2.46	3.07	3.82	4.74	5.87
24	1.61	2.03	2.56	3.23	4.05	5.07	6.34
25	1.64	2.09	2.67	3.39	4.29	5.43	6.85
26	1.67	2.16	2.77	3.56	4.55	5.81	7.40
27	1.71	2.22	2.88	3.73	4.82	6.21	7.99
28	1.74	2.29	3.00	3.92	5.11	6.65	8.63
29	1.78	2.36	3.12	4.12	5.42	7.11	9.32
30	1.81	2.43	3.24	4.32	5.74	7.61	10.06

Summary Income Planning Worksheet

Year	Monthly Needs & Wamts*	Wages or Self-Empl.	Social Security	Pensions and Annuities	Retirement Plan Payouts	Savings and Invest.	**Total Monthly Income**
1							
2							
3							
4							
5							
6							
7							
8							
9							
10							
11							
12							
13							
14							
15							
16							
17							
18							
19							
20							
21							
22							
23							
24							
25							
26							
27							
28							
29							
30							

* Inflation-adjusted

Chapter 10

••••••••••••••

Why Seniors Should Plan for Long-Term Care

According to a study published in *The New England Journal of Medicine*, 33% of all men and 50% of all women over age 65 will face a need for long-term care at some point. Women are at somewhat greater risk than men because they live longer and are more likely to be single at older ages.

In 2004, the average national cost of staying in a nursing home for one year was about $55,000. For care at either an individual's home or in an assisted living facility, the costs ranged from $25,000 to $60,000 per year. However, in some areas, costs are higher. In New York State, for example, skilled nursing facilities have averaged about $75,000 per year. In New York City and surrounding suburbs, however, the cost can exceed $90,000 per year.

For these reasons, seniors should increase their knowledge about long-term care and how to protect against it, and now is the best time to start. By planning ahead, you can integrate long-term care protection into your retirement planning and avoid losing a large part of your assets to nursing home costs. You also can gain confidence that you won't b ecome a burden on family or friends.

Levels of Care

Most long-term care is "custodial" in nature, which means that it doesn't require a doctor's supervision or skilled nursing care. Instead, it offers assistance with "activities of daily living" (ADLs) on a continuing basis. Some examples of ADLs include bathing, dressing, eating and moving about.

On a per diem basis, hospitals cost far more than long-term care. Most hospital visits last a few weeks, at most, and costs usually are covered by private health insurance or Medicare. The need for long-term care can last years, and only a small part of the cost usually is covered by any insurance or government program other than Medicaid.

Most long-term care is delivered in the home by family or friends, especially when the need is for "stand-by assistance," the lowest level of custodial care. Stand-by means that someone is available to monitor the person who needs care. The next higher levels involve "directional assistance," which means guidance in performing ADLs, and "substantial assistance," which lends hands-on help in eating, bathing or moving about. Often, a willing and able spouse can provide stand-by or directional assistance. According to the American Health Planning Association, about 75% of all long-term care is provided by family members.

The highest level of care is "skilled nursing care," which includes substantial assistance plus the giving of medications and other professional medical services. Medicare only pays for skilled nursing care, in most cases.

Who Is Available to Provide Care?

The need for a nursing home, however, involves more than the level of care. Just as important is the issue of who will provide the care and in what setting. Elderly men who need care often have spouses available to assist them. Since elderly women are more likely to survive spouses and live alone, they may not have the same luxury. Some medical conditions, such as Alzheimer's, produce steady deterioration inthe ability to perform ADLs and an increased need for care over time. Even if families are able to provide home care in the early stages, they may grow exhausted by the responsibility over time.

Currently, nursing home costs in the U.S. average about $125 to $175 per day (depending on geographic region), or about $45,000 to $65,000 per year. The costs tend to be higher in cities than rural areas and they are somewhat greater on the East and West coasts than in the Midwest or South. An Alternative Living Facility (ALF) offers independent, community-based living at a cost that can be 20–30% cheaper than nursing homes, due to a lower level of supervision and care.

A home health aide or nurse attendant can be a viable option for some people, if finances allow. Having a skilled nurse visit a home three times a week, for two hours per visit, can cost $15,000 to $20,000 per year — less than half the cost of a nursing home. A home health aide hired on the same basis can cost about $10,000 per year. Neither private insurance nor Medicare are likely to reimburse these costs unless skilled nursing care is required following a hospital stay. Even then, reimbursements may continue only for brief periods.

Who Pays for Long-Term Care?

Until age 65, most people's health insurance is either privately purchased or provided (in whole or part) by an employer, union or association. Beginning at age 65, most Americans enroll in Medicare, the federal government's insurance program for seniors. Because it is widely available and economical compared to private health coverage, Medicare is used by the vast majority of seniors.

Currently, Medicare has about 40 million participants, most of whom pay $78.20 per month (in 2005) for the "Part B" premium that covers doctor's bills. Part A, which covers hospital bills, is free to eligible seniors with 40 or more covered quarters starting at age 65. Both parts of Medicare also contain a variety of co-pays and deductibles, but much of their costs can be covered by purchasing private Medicare supplement insurance ("Medigap"), which is sold in 10 standard plans.

The most costly myth about health insurance for seniors is the idea that the combination of Medicare and Medigap creates a strong health insurance "safety net." If there is such a safety net, it contains a large hole through which most or all of a senior's life savings can disappear in a short time. This hole exists because neither Medicare nor Medigap cover most costs of long-term care.

What Long-Term Care Does Medicare Cover?

The highest level of long-term care is called "skilled nursing care," and it is usually administered in a specialized medical facility under a doctor's supervision. Medicare may cover up to 20 days of treatment at a skilled nursing care facility at full cost, plus part of the cost of another 80 days. All except two of the 10 Medigap standard plans include a skilled nursing coinsurance that covers most of the balance during those 80 days. Of course, there's a catch. If Medicare declines to cover any part of those 80 days, Medigap plans won't fill the gaps, either.

Medicare pays for a nursing home only in very limited situations involving hospital stays, doctors' orders and a skilled nursing need. Four of the standard Medigap plans include an at-home recovery benefit that may reimburse part of the costs of a skilled nurse or home health aide. But this coverage is limited to assistance with ADLs following an illness, injury or surgery, and it lasts a relatively short time.

In summary, Medicare and Medigap can't be relied upon to pay most of the cost of long-term care in a nursing home, community-based facility or private home — especially if the treatment lasts a long time.

Medicaid and The Elderly Indigent

The bulk of long-term care cost falls on two funding sources: Medicaid and the savings of the elderly. Medicaid, a welfare program jointly funded by the federal government and the states, supports long-term care for the elderly indigent. In recent years, Medicaid has funded approximately half of the total costs of nursing homes in the U.S. But the catch is that you must qualify to have nursing home bills paid by Medicaid, and that usually means spending down virtually all your assets, except for the value of a primary residence. Also, you must agree to receive care in a Medicaid-approved facility.

Patching The Hole in The Safety Net

Long-term care insurance (LTCI) has become a bedrock financial solution for protecting retirement savings against the rising cost of long-term care. Think of LTCI as working together with Medicare and Medigap coverage to make the health insurance safety nets of seniors strong. Planning for this coverage, and including its premium cost in retirement budgets, can be among the most important steps in protecting your standard of living, while increasing your confidence that all your hard work and planning won't be devastated by an illness, injury or the recovery period. This coverage also adds to your confidence that you won't become a burden on others, and that your other important financial goals—such as leaving money to your children or grandchildren—will be met.

The best way to start planning for long-term care is to learn how to evaluate LTCI programs intelligently. The next chapter is designed to help you.

Chapter 11

••••••••••••••

How to Make Long-Term Care Insurance Affordable

What's different about financial planning today compared to 20 years ago? An important addition is an LTCI policy used to provide for a nursing home stay or extended care at home. This insurance coverage currently is offered by about 15–20 leading life/health insurance companies in the United States.

When considering the purchase of an LTCI program, sooner is better because premiums are more affordable when the program begins at younger ages. If you are considering LTCI for yourself or a loved one, the ideas below can help you select a program that is both effective and affordable.

LTCI Choices That Impact Costs

Four choices in an LTCI program canimpact the premium cost:

1. **The maximum daily benefit** paid by the insurance company for each day of care. This varies from about $50 to $250 per day.

2. **The maximum payout period** during which the insurance company continues benefit payments. This varies from two years to unlimited.

3. **The "waiting period"** during which long-term care is delivered but the insurance company does not pay. This varies from zero to 90 days of costs you must pay out-of-pocket before benefits begin.

4. Whether the daily benefit **increases each year to account for inflation**. A typical inflation adjustment is 5% per year.

Smart-Shopping Ideas

One way to start shopping is to research costs of long-term care facilities in your area, including nursing homes and assisted living facilities (ALFs). For example, a facility with an annual cost of $60,000 would require a daily benefit of $164 per day, assuming you want to avoid any out-of-pocket costs (after the waiting period). If you could afford to pay part of this cost yourself, without depleting your savings, you might reduce the premium cost by choosing a daily benefit below $164.

It's generally not a good idea to economize by choosing a shorter payment period. According to one study, four of the leading causes of long-term care are Alzheimer's, diabetes, cancer and stroke. The average length of care required is 96 months for Alzheimer's, 48 months for diabetes, 36 months for cancer and 21 months for a stroke. So, it's smart to select a payment period of five years or longer.

While you can save premium costs by declining an annual inflation adjustment, this also could become costly. One study projected that the average cost of nursing home care will keep increasing and reach $90,000 per year within the next decade. Even two or three years of care costing $90,000 would wreck the finances of many retired people, unless they have LTCI with automatic annual increases.

Perhaps the best way to shop wisely for LTCI is to work with a financial professional who can help you compare benefits and costs with sensitivity for your budget. It's never too early to begin discussing the need for LTCI, because planning ahead and starting your program at a younger age can reduce the annual premium cost for the rest of your life. The same ideas can be effective in helping a parent choose an LTCI program, too.

Ideas to Help You Select an LTCI Program

1. **Evaluate the financial strength of the life insurance company.** LTCI programs are only as strong as the life insurance company's ability to honor its guarantees and pay benefits. Studies have shown that the average age at which nursing home confinement begins is 78, so the company must be capable of

meeting claims for decades. Begin your analysis by evaluating ratings of the company's financial strength, as published by leading agencies such as Bests, Standard & Poor's, Moodys and Weiss.

2. **Evaluate the potential for stable future rates.** By law, no company or agent can claim that future costs for LTCI are guaranteed. Just remember that some companies have years of experience in this field, combined with traditions of keeping premium rates relatively stable for existing policyholders. You want to make sure your coverage remains affordable until you need it. So, check and see if companies have raised rates in your state in recent years.

3. **Insist on a "qualified" program.** Congress defined tax-qualified LTCI programs in the Health Insurance Portability & Accountability Act of 1996 (HIPAA). In a qualified program, benefit payments are federally income tax-free up to a limit. Also, premium payments are tax-deductible on a similar basis with other health insurance programs. Since a qualified program must meet government standards to become certified, it has earned the equivalent of a seal of approval in regard to quality of care.

4. **Require guaranteed renewability.** Like permanent life insurance policies, LTCI is designed to last the rest of your life. The program you choose should guarantee that coverage will be renewed each year for as long as you live, regardless of your age or health.

5. **Select a compounding, automatic annual increase.** Most programs offer you an option of having the maximum benefit automatically increased each year to offset inflation, and there is a big difference between having your benefits increase at a "compound" rate each year vs. a "simple" rate. For example, suppose your program starts with a maximum benefit of $150 per day of care and increases 5% per year. After 20 years, a compounding increase will pay up to $398 per day, while a simple increase will pay only $300.

6. **Evaluate enhanced benefits.** Some LTCI programs offer enhanced benefits either as standard features or options available at modestly higher cost. For example, you may qualify for "good health discounts" if you exercise regularly and don't smoke. Two married people applying at the same time may qualify for an additional "couple's discount." Some programs pay a death benefit if you die without receiving any benefits, and another valuable feature is a "true return of premium" to a named beneficiary, if the insured person dies without receiving benefit payments.

7. **Avoid limited coverage.** Some policies explicitly exclude specific types of illnesses that can require lengthy periods of care, including Alzheimer's and Parkinson's. Another limitation to avoid is a requirement of "prior hospitalization" before qualifying for benefits.

8. **Choose full coverage.** The best programs cover three types of care: nursing home, community-facility based and home health care. Beware of programs that cover home health care only under narrowly defined circumstances, such as when a skilled nurse is required or following a hospital stay. You should have the option of choosing home-based treatment if that best meets your needs, including informal care from an unlicensed provider (a "caretaker").

9. **Make sure the promises match the fine print.** Every LTCI program has different features that can only be understood by reading the fine print of the contract. Since this is a long-term commitment, it's a good idea to have a trusted family member and perhaps an attorney go over the contract, too, prior to purchase. Sales promises don't mean much if they don't match the fine print.

Chapter 12

•••••••••••••

The Advantages of "Blended" Solutions

The LTCI industry has encountered a problem in recent years, and it's the same problem that all other segments of the health care industry have faced: rising costs. Initially, LTCI was designed so that premiums could stay level over many years, if not for life. This design worked well for seniors living on fixed incomes. Also, since seniors could lock in lower level premiums at younger ages, it made sense for them to buy LTCI at the onset of retirement, if not before.

Now, however, it appears that many companies that issue LTCI will not be able to hold premiums level, and this cost uncertainty has seniors very concerned. They are asking: "What good is it to lock in a low premium by 'buying early' if the costs will skyrocket at older ages? And what happens if costs go so high that I can't afford LTCI at all?"

The insurance industry is answering these questions with new LTCI product designs that offer "unbundled choices" designed to keep premiums affordable. For example, Blue Cross has introduced a plan, LTC blue, that lets the insured mix different levels of coverage, such as 100% for nursing homes, 75% for ALFs and 50% for home care. (In this example, if the maximum monthly benefit is $4,000 for a nursing home, it would be $3,000 for an ALF and $2,000 for home care.) LTC blue's "Nursing Home Only" option offers a 0% benefit for ALFs or home care.

We advise our clients to be careful with unbundled solutions, due to the intricate process of placing an elderly person in an long-term care program. The process can involve months of coordination among medical and mental health professionals, social services organizations, family members and financial advisors. Ultimately, the placement may depend on compatibility and availability — where the elderly person feels most comfortable among affordable programs with capacity. I don't want to see a situation in which, years from now, a client needs and wants home care instead of a nursing home, but can't afford that choice because he/she bought an LTCI program with a 0% benefit for home health care. You don't know what level or type of long-term care you will need years from now, or what type of program will be compatible and available. So, why try to guess in choosing an LTCI product?

Prepaying Long-Term Care Costs

If program's like Blue Cross's aren't the best answer to rising LTCI costs, what is? For some clients, I believe an attractive solution can be to prepay long-term care costs with a one-time premium, while bundling guaranteed lifetime coverage into life insurance. In one package, for one payment, you can get:

- Life insurance coverage
- Long-term care protection
- Tax-deferred accumulation of cash value
- Access to cash value (if needed) through withdrawals

This package of benefits is available in a variety of "blended" single-pay life insurance products with accelerated death benefits for long-term care. In one policy, and with one premium payment, you can blend both life insurance and long-term care protection.

How Blended Policies Work

How do these solutions work? If you develop either a terminal or chronic illness, they will accelerate all or most of your life insurance death benefit to cover long-term care costs. For example, a chronic illness might be claimed if you are certified to need help with two or more ADLs. Then, after a waiting period in any type of long-term care program (nursing home, ALF or home care) you could begin receiving about 2% of your death benefit per month for up to 40–50 months. Every dollar of death benefit that you accelerate reduces the amount payable to your life insurance beneficiary at death by a dollar. Eventually, if you stay in the nursing home for more than 40–50 months, you would deplete the policy's death benefit and coverage.

You can purchase a blended, single-pay contract from several companies for premiums as low as $10,000. But to have enough coverage to protect yourself against a lengthy need for long-term care, you probably should put $50,000 or more into the program. Since this is the only payment required, and terms are contractually guaranteed by the life insurance company, your costs can't increase. Also, your $50,000 would purchase an immediate death benefit (and long-term care protection amount) that is somewhat greater than the premium, depending on your age and sex. The ratio of your death benefit to your single payment is higher for younger people than older folks, and it is higher for women than men (because women outlive men and their mortality risk is less).

Affordable Long-Term Care Protection

Whichever side of the blended protection you don't use (life insurance or long-term care) winds up costing you very little. For example, if you never need the long-term care, you still have your death benefit intact, and the long-term care protection becomes economical.

Also, I believe there is a flexibility benefit built into these policies. To understand it, imagine a family that must fund long-term care for grandma at age 80, when grandma has Alzheimer's and also a $200,000 blended policy death benefit that can be accelerated. The family can help grandma decide to either: 1) keep the death benefit intact for heirs and fund the long-term care out-of-pocket; or 2) accelerate the benefit and apply it to long-term care. It's an option you don't have if you buy regular LTCI.

One big attraction of "blended," single-pay policies is in the leverage they offer older women. Women are statistically more likely to need long-term care than men because they live longer and are less likely to have caregivers at home. To illustrate this leverage, imagine a 70-year-old woman who puts a $100,000 single premium into one attractive, blended product. Her leverage factor is 1.70, which means every dollar of payment immediately earns $1.70 of death benefit. Since this product accelerates up to 90% of death benefit, $100,000 of premium would leverage into $153,000 of long-term care coverage — enough to pay for about 2–3 years in a nursing home or 3–4 years in an ALF. (For a male age 70, the same premium would buy a bit less long-term care coverage, about $140,000.)

Some companies will write this type of product up to age 85 for premiums as low as $10,000. Also, the company may guarantee that cash value will earn a minimum interest rate. The only problem with some blended policies is that the accelerated death benefit is not yet approved in some states, including New York.

If you are concerned about the potential for rising or uncertain LTCI costs, I urge you to take a look at blended programs with accelerated death benefits available in your state. At The Senior Financial Center, we'll be happy to help you.

Chapter 13

•••••••••••••

An Overview of Social Security Benefits

At The Senior Financial Center, we have a number of clients in their 80s. Most of them have been collecting Social Security retirement benefits for approximately 15–25 years. Social Security checks have become part of the fabric of their retirement lives, so they more or less assume the Social Security system has been around forever.

It comes as a surprise to some of these people to learn that they are older than Social Security. The system was created during the presidency of Franklin Roosevelt, who signed Social Security into law on August 14, 1935. Social Security was the biggest and historically most important part of Roosevelt's "New Deal," a collection of government-administered programs designed to help the United States escape the crushing poverty of the Great Depression. At the time Social Security was enacted, the U.S. had approximately seven million people age 65 or older, roughly 5% of the population.

On January 31, 1940, Ida M. Fuller, a legal secretary from Ludlow, Vermont, became the first person to receive a monthly retirement benefit check under Social Security. She had paid a total of $44 in taxes into the Social Security system and her first check was for $22.54. Yet, Ms. Fuller lived another 35 years, to age 100, and collected a total of $20,884.52 in benefits before she passed away.

The Value of Historical Perspective

I think it's important to put Social Security into historical perspective, especially for today's seniors who have lived through the system's formative years. The original goal of Social Security was to offer a relatively small number of retired people over age 65 (just 5% of the population) a basic level of financial security through a modest insurance benefit. Even back in 1940, $22.54 per month didn't buy much.

But the first recipient of Social Security—who far outlived her life expectancy and received hundreds of times more benefits than she paid in taxes — set the stage for massive changes that were to come. All of these changes have occurred during your lifetime:

- In 1940, there were 112,000 retired workers in the U.S. who qualified for Social Security retirement benefits. Today, these benefits are paid to more than 25 million Americans.

- In 1940, the maximum benefit payable at full retirement age was $41.20 per month. Today, it is more than $1,500 per month.

- Through 1949, the maximum contribution payable into the system by employees was just $30 per year. In 2004, a self-employed person could have paid as much as $10,900 in Social Security payroll taxes, plus additional amounts for Medicare.

- Since its origin, Social Security has issued 415 million identification numbers and paid out a total of more than $7 trillion in cash benefits.

Social Security has become an enormous enterprise that is very costly to working people (in FICA or self-employment taxes) and very important to retired people wishing to maintain their standards of living. But despite the bigger numbers, the fundamental role of this program hasn't changed much in your lifetime. It still is designed to provide only a base level of retirement financial security — nothing more.

I strongly advise our clients to understand their options and rights in regard to Social Security retirement benefits, while considering them as just one leg in the four-legged chair of total retirement income. The other three legs are:

1. Retirement plans and IRAs

2. Pension and annuity income

3. Your other personal savings and investments

In the rest of this chapter, I'll explain the process of building Social

Security benefits into a total retirement income plan, while making smart choices as to when retirement benefits should start. I'll also discuss how Social Security benefits are taxed. In the next chapter, I will offer my best thinking on how the Social Security benefits formula could change over the next 20–40 years, due to well-publicized, long-term weaknesses in the system's finances.

What You Earn

Social Security retirement benefits are calculated in one of two ways:

1. What you earn yourself as a wage-earner, based on your salary or self-employed earnings in your 35 highest earning years (as indexed). You need 40 calendar quarters (10 years) of covered employment to be fully insured in the system.

2. What you earn as the spouse of a wage-earner, assuming you were married to a qualifying worker for at least 10 years. A spouse earns half of the worker's benefits, assuming that benefits begin at the age of full benefits (see table below).

    Note: The Social Security system also pays benefits to disabled workers and widows, widowers, and dependents of deceased or disabled workers.

Social Security automatically calculates your benefits both ways and will pay you the higher of these two amounts when you decide to begin benefits, which can be as early as age 62.

How much can you expect to receive? All workers who pay into Social Security receive a *Social Security Statement* annually, approximately every three months before their birthdays. This *Statement* contains a detailed history of your earnings record and an estimate of the income you can expect to receive at retirement. As you approach age 62, it's also a good idea to call your local Social Security office. Or, you can call a national, toll-free number (1-800-772-1213) for information and income planning assistance.

You qualify to receive full Social Security retirement benefits at a given age, and this age is scheduled to increase in the future, as shown in the table on the next page.

Age to Receive Full Social Security Benefits

If you were born in...	Age to receive full benefits
1937 or earlier	65
1938	65 and 2 months
1939	65 and 4 months
1940	65 and 6 months
1941	65 and 8 months
1942	65 and 10 months
1943–1954	66
1955	66 and 2 months
1956	66 and 4 months
1957	66 and 6 months
1958	66 and 8 months
1959	66 and 10 months
1960 or later	67

You may start benefits as early as age 62. But for every month in which you begin before the age shown above (for your birth year), you will permanently lose a part of your benefits. For example, the table on the next page shows how much people born between 1943 and 1954 will lose by "starting benefits early."

How Social Security Benefits Are Reduced

If you were born betweem 1943 and 1954 and start benefits at age...	And you are the...	
	Wage-Earner	**Spouse**
	Your retirement benefit is reduced to...	
62	75.0%	35.0%
62 + 6 months	77.5%	36.3%
63	80.0%	37.5%
63 + 6 months	83.3%	39.6%
64	86.7%	41.7%
64 + 6 months	90.0%	43.8%
65	93.3%	45.8%
65 + 6 months	96.7%	47.9%
66	100.0%	50.0%

Example: You are a wage-earner born in 1945. Based on your highest 35 earning years, you could expect a benefit of $1,400 per month if you begin at age 66. Your spouse could earn a benefit of $700 per month if he/she begins at age 66. Your combined monthly income starting at age 66 would be $2,100. But suppose you both start benefits at age 62 instead of waiting until 66. In that case, you would receive 75% of $1,400 per month and your spouse would receive 70% of $700 per month. The total would be $1,540. By starting at age 62 instead of 66, you would permanently lose the difference between $2,100 and $1,540, which is $560 per month.

Should You Start Early?

When seniors ask if they should start benefits early, we in turn ask them three basic questions:

- What do you need the "starting early" money for?
- What rate of interest could you get if you saved the money?
- How long do you expect to live?

Some people really need the extra income that they could get from early Social Security benefits. For example, they may be forced to pay their own medical insurance premiums until qualifying for Medicare at age 65. Or, they may have pensions kicking in at age 65 and need income to "fill the gap."

If you are saving the money you get from Social Security between ages 62 and 65–66, then it might make sense to "start early" when interest rates are high. You might save more money with compound interest that you would give up in future benefits. Remember that when you consider the "time value of money," a dollar in hand today is worth more than a dollar to be received the future. A detailed "present value analysis" of your particular situation could help you decide.

To understand the third question, it helps to understand what may be the most valuable feature of Social Security — especially if you plan to live a long time. That is the Cost of Living Adjustment (COLA) written into current law, which automatically increases benefits annually based on changes in the Consumer Price Index. The COLA has been in effect since 1975, and the table on the next page shows the historic COLAs that have been granted.

Social Security Cost-of-Living Adjustments

Year	COLA	Year	COLA
1975	8.0%	1990	5.4%
1976	6.4%	1991	3.7%
1977	5.9%	1992	3.0%
1978	6.5%	1993	2.6%
1979	9.9%	1994	2.8%
1980	14.3%	1995	2.6%
1981	11.2%	1996	2.9%
1982	7.4%	1997	2.1%
1983	3.5%	1998	1.3%
1984	3.5%	1999	2.5%
1985	3.1%	2000	3.5%
1986	1.3%	2001	2.6%
1987	4.2%	2002	1.4%
1988	4.0%	2003	2.1%
1989	4.7%		

If you had started Social Security benefits in 1975 at $500 per month, you would have received $1,160 per month in 2003 thanks to the annual COLA increases. The longer you expect to live, the more valuable future COLA benefits will be to you, assuming no changes in the law. To estimate your odds of outliving a normal life expectancy, see Chapter 18.

The COLA and Longevity Protection

Of the four legs in your retirement income chair, Social Security is the only one that may be increased automatically each year to offset inflation, for as long as you live. That's why it can pay to maximize your Social Security benefits by starting the year you qualify for full benefits (or later). For each month that you delay the start of benefits after that year, you can earn credits for delayed retirement that will permanently increase your benefits, as shown in the table below.

Increase for Delayed Retirement

Year of Birth	Yearly Rate of Increase
1930	4.5%
1931–1932	5.0%
1933–1934	5.5%
1935–1936	6.0%
1937–1938	6.5%
1939–1940	7.0%
1941–1942	7.5%
1943 or later	8.0%

Example: Suppose that both the husband and spouse in the previous example (both born in 1945) delayed benefits by one year and started at age 67. In that case, they would receive a permanent increase equal to 8.0% more than the $2,100 in combined benefits they would have received at age 66, plus any COLA that applied in the year of delay.

In summary, the three main points to keep in mind about your Social Security benefits are these:

1. Social Security was never meant to provide all the financial security you need in retirement. Consider it just one leg of four.

2. The major advantage that the Social Security leg offers, under current law, is the fact that benefits are increased each year to offset Consumer Price Index inflation, through the COLA.

3. The longer you live and collect benefits, the more valuable the COLA will be, assuming it isn't changed in the future.

For my views on whether and how Social Security benefits might be changed in the future, see the next chapter.

Tax on Your Social Security Benefits

Until 1983, seniors did not pay any federal income tax on Social Security benefits. In 1983, when Ronald Reagan was president, the law was changed, so that up to 50% of benefits could be subject to income tax for single filers with combined incomes above $25,000 or joint filers above $32,000. For purposes of this calculation, "combined income" was defined as:

- Adjusted gross income

- Tax-exempt bond interest

- Half of Social Security benefits

The tax collections resulting from this income were transferred to Social Security trust funds.

In 1993, a second tier of tax on Social Security was added, using the same formula for calculating "combined income." This tier begins at combined income of $34,000 for single filers and $44,000 for joint filers, and it can include up to 85% of Social Security benefits in taxable income. (The extra tax collections the government receives on this tier are allocated for the Medicare [HI] trust fund.)

Examples:

Helen is a single filer with combined income of $32,000. She falls above the first tier but below the second. So, up to 50% of her Social Security benefits could be taxable. She avoids having up to 85% of her benefits being taxable, because she falls below the second tier.

David and Joan are joint filers with combined income of $60,000. They fall above both tiers and could have up to 85% of their benefits taxed.

Three Key Points

There are three key points that seniors should understand about taxation of their Social Security benefits.

1. Your tax bracket may be higher than you think. Your actual federal tax bracket (the highest effective rate that you pay on a dollar of income) may actually be above the rate shown in published IRS tables. This occurs because in certain ranges of income, an extra dollar of income is taxed in its own right and also causes either 50 cents or an additional 35 cents Social Security benefits to become taxable.

2. Tax-exempt municipal bond interest isn't always totally tax-free for Social Security recipients. A dollar of tax-exempt interest can, in some cases, cause either 50 cents or an additional 35 cents of Social Security benefits to become taxable.

3. Tax-deferred annuities, tax-advantaged life insurance contracts and retirement plans can help seniors avoid having more of their benefits taxed.

It's not always easy for seniors to estimate how much tax they will owe each year due to the complexity of Social Security taxes. Ideally, you should consult with a tax advisor in the last few months of each year and see if you can take more current income without causing more of your Social Security to become taxable. In a tax-deferred annuity, for example, you can take taxable withdrawals of exactly the amount of money that you need. You also could obtain this money as a distribution from your IRAs or as a tax-free loan from a permanent life insurance contract.

You also may want to consider the tax on Social Security in your decision regarding when to start benefits.

Chapter 14

•••••••••••••

The Future of Social Security

Social Security is often called the "third rail" of American politics. This means that it's about as safe for a politician to bring up an idea for reforming the Social Security system as it is to touch the high-voltage third rail of an electrified train system.

The reality is that Social Security has a fundamental long-term financing problem on its hands. As millions of Baby Boomers start retiring and living to very old ages, fewer workers will be paying taxes into the system each year to support a growing population of retired people.

Eventually, changes must be made or the system will run out of money. In 2004, the Social Security Trustees reported that the system is projected to spend more money than it receives in tax collections starting in 2018. Then, in another 22 years (by 2042), the system is projected to exhaust its Old Age, Survivors and Disability Income (OASDI) trust fund (i.e. run out of money). Currently, that trust fund has $1.5 trillion in assets. But over the next 75 years, the system is projected to require an estimated $3.7 trillion in today's dollars to meet all obligations to retirees and other beneficiaries (mainly survivors and the disabled).

It's a sobering long-term picture that all retired people (and those soon to retire) should open their eyes and see. Changes are in store for Social Security long-term. But what are those changes likely to be — and how can you plan for them? In this chapter, I'll give you my best ideas and strategies, boiled down to six main points.

1. **The Social Security battle lines have already been drawn, and they aren't political.** They are generational, with a dividing line somewhere around age 50, where AARP membership begins.

It's important to recognize that "the AARP crowd" is potentially among the most powerful political forces in U.S. history. Until now, Americans over age 50 have not yet been unified behind any single political party or cause. But I believe their unity will grow in the future behind the need to protect Social Security benefits. The older segment of this crowd, those currently age 70 and above, have already come to depend on Social Security for at least part of their retirement security — and they don't want to give it up. The younger segment of this crowd, ages 50–70, have another motive for protecting their benefits — namely, the small fortunes they have paid into the system over their full work careers. Due to changes in the payroll tax formula enacted in the past quarter century, younger retirees, on average, have paid into the system three to five times as much as older retirees. It seems unjust to this generation, now retiring or approaching retirement, that they should have paid such high taxes to support Social Security and then see their benefits cut.

2. **The political clout of the elderly means that any future changes in the Social Security benefits formula probably will be gradual.** For example, several economic leaders, including Federal Reserve Chairman Alan Greenspan, have advocated a change in the formula for calculating the annual COLA. Although this change is fairly minor and technical, knocking a decimal point or two off the COLA each year could save billions of dollars for the system long term. For planning purposes, people who are nearing retirement today might prudently assume that approximately 80% to 90% of today's estimated benefits will actually be received after the necessary reforms are made. (AARP says the system is projected to have enough money to pay 100% of current benefits through 2042 and 75% thereafter.)

3. **The "privatization" model advocated for Social Security by some politicians will be a struggle to achieve.** "Privatization" would allow workers to set up personal accounts with a bank, brokerage firm, mutual fund or insurance company and divert part of their payroll taxes into private accounts. It sounds like a good idea to some people — but don't hold your breath!

The Social Security Administration's statement on this subject is as follows: "There are no credible plans to replace Social Security as the foundation for the retirement of American workers." However, it is possible that younger workers eventually will have an option of diverting some of their payroll taxes into "personal accounts" administered by Social Security.

4. **Social Security has fallen behind the times.** As the average age for starting retirement has declined, the age for receiving full Social Security retirement benefits is on a steady rise, as discussed in the previous chapter. Many people currently in their late 50s or early 60s will experience a "gap period" that starts when they stop working full-time and ends around age 66, when full Social Security retirement benefits can begin. It's important for these people to create income strategies capable of filling the "gap years." Many income-generating solutions discussed elsewhere in this book can be useful in filling temporary income gaps.

5. **Social Security provides a shrinking part of the retirement financial security that affluent Americans need.** According to the Social Security Administration, retirement benefits provide 38% of the total retirement income of Americans age 65 and above. But for the more affluent segment, that portion is below 25%. Even if the benefits formula doesn't change in the future, the relative importance of Social Security in retirement planning will continue to shrink, according to a research study conducted by the Center for Retirement Research at Boston College. Over the next 30 years, the portion of pre-retirement income that Social Security replaces will decline by about 5% due to factors integrated into current law.

One proposed solution to the long-term shortfall involves increasing the taxable portion of Social Security to 100% for affluent retirees and crediting increased tax collections to the trust fund. Since this wouldn't involve direct benefits cuts and would have the greatest impact on high-income people, it could become politically acceptable, although it would further erode the portion of after-tax retirement income on which affluent older Americans rely.

6. **Seniors should focus retirement planning on what they can control, not complex Social Security issues that will take years to resolve through solutions now unfathomable.** In short, it doesn't

pay to dwell on speculation about what actions politicians may (or may not) take years from now. Build your retirement planning process so that it can withstand minor and gradual reductions in the current Social Security benefit formula. The higher your retirement standard of living is — the less you may want to count on future Social Security benefits.

The longer you expect to live, the more likely it is that you will live through changes in the current Social Security system. Eventually, politicians will have to touch that third rail — or else the whole country will go broke. That's not going to happen, so here is a scenario that suggests what might:

- Around 2010, Congress could change the COLA formula so that benefits don't quite keep pace with inflation. Lawmakers also could create a "sliding COLA" that decreases at higher incomes.

- Around the same time (or a few years later), Congress may make all Social Security benefits taxable for the affluent — and allocate these tax collections to the trust fund.

- Around 2010 to 2015, younger workers might be given the option of allocating a portion of their payroll taxes to personal accounts administered by Social Security — in return for lower promised benefits.

- Around 2020, benefits might be reduced or capped for taxpayers reporting taxable incomes above a given amount, such as $200,000.

Changes this gradual aren't going to hurt you too much or wreck your retirement planning — provided you haven't built your whole retirement income so that it depends on Social Security.

Chapter 15

•••••••••••••

Annuities: Don't Believe Everything You Read

When you are learning about annuities, don't always believe everything you hear or read in the media. Here's why I offer this advice.

When I meet "strangers," they usually don't stay strangers for long, of course. In the first moments that we are getting acquainted, I may ask them two questions:

1. Have you ever owned annuities?

2. What is your view of annuities in general — positive, negative or indifferent?

Here is what I often find:

1. People who have never owned annuities usually have a negative or indifferent view of them.

2. But people who have actually owned annuities usually report a positive experience — in line with their expectations or better.

Over time, the reason for this difference in opinion has become apparent. The first group, lacking direct experience, has had to form views about annuities by relying on the media or friends. The second group has the benefit of personal experience.

Media Sour Grapes

For years, it seems the media, in general, has been very negative about annuities and their benefits, especially for seniors. For example, on February 9, 1998, *Forbes* magazine ran a feature article called "The Great Annuity Rip-Off." The article said, in part:

"Recent tax law changes should have wiped out sales of variable annuities, but they are as hot as ever. How gullible can investors get?"

Here's what *Kipplinger's* said about annuities in its issue of August 1999:

"Tax-deferred variable annuities...have drawbacks for older investors. You won't come out ahead for years. To overcome high costs, you may have to leave the earnings in the annuity a decade or more."

Those are just two of many negative press accounts that I've collected over the years. Why has the media consistently been so negative about tax-deferred annuities in general, especially variable annuities? After a lot of thought, I've come up with two possible answers.

1. Many people who work in the media and write these articles may never have owned annuities.

2. The media has focused at least 90% of its coverage on only one side of the annuity market and annuity-owning experience: tax-deferred annuities, which are designed for the accumulating phase. Later in this book, I'll discuss the pros and cons of tax-deferred annuities. Also, there is another important type of annuity that can be very advantageous for some seniors. It is called either an "income annuity" or an "immediate annuity." Also included in this type is a tax-deferred annuity that is converted into an income annuity as you pass from your accumulation phase into your preservation/income phase. This process is called "annuitization." For reasons I'll never understand, the media has practically ignored this very important side of the annuity discussion.

Here's a story that may help to explain how valuable annuities can be for seniors. Pauline was a widow age 74 living on her Social Security and a small amount of CD income. There were two things about Pauline you would not know, unless you were among her best friends. First, she owned more than 60 acres of undeveloped farmland that she had inherited years before. Second, she was in absolutely top health, and both her parents had lived to about age 90.

When Pauline sold her farmland to a developer, she realized a long-term capital gain of a little more than $700,000. After taxes, she had approximately $600,000 left. What Pauline wanted to know was the same thing you might want to know if you had this kind of windfall: Was she really wealthy? Could she afford to travel and take cruises all over the world? Did she now have enough money to support herself in style for the rest of her life, even if she lived to 100 or older?

This happened a few years ago, when interest rates were very low and short-term CDs were paying about 2%. So, when Pauline considered the income her $600,000 would produce each year in CDs — about $12,000 — she didn't feel wealthy. In fact, she didn't even think she could afford to change her lifestyle much.

Immediate annuities were an attractive option for Pauline for three basic reasons:

1.   Her most important goal was to generate a guaranteed income that she would not outlive.

2.   She was in excellent health and there was a good chance she **would live a very long time**.

3.   Immediate annuities offered an opportunity to increase her standard of living by producing more current income than any other guaranteed alternative.

For Pauline, the best choice was a "life income with 10-year certain" payout from an annuity issued by a high-quality life insurance company. You'll learn more about the different payout options in the next chapter. With this choice, she was able to generate a guaranteed income of approximately $45,000 per year, of which more than 80% was received income tax-free. Well, I'm happy to tell you that Pauline is still alive and healthy, and part of that is the mental health of knowing a guaranteed income will continue as long as she lives, and she'll never need to depend on anyone financially. For her, that was the real key to feeling richer and living better.

But, of course, the media did not report Pauline's story, or that of so many other seniors who have had similar satisfying experiences with annuities.

Five Basic Questions and The Answers

I ask you to clear your mind of all the clutter that you've read about annuities and start over from the beginning with the facts. First, let me answer five basic questions that my clients often ask.

1. What is an annuity?

An annuity is a contractual agreement between the buyer and a life insurance company. The buyer puts money into the annuity in either a lump sum or a series of payments. The company agrees to pay out an income that may begin either immediately (in an immediate annuity) or at a later date (in a tax-deferred annuity). In most cases, the income is paid to the person who is named the contract's "annuitant," and this usually is the same person as the buyer/owner. In many contracts, two people may be named as "joint annuitants." Often, annuity income is guaranteed by the company from the time the first payment is made until the annuitant dies or until the second of two joint annuitants dies. It is also possible to select a guaranteed income payout over a defined period of years (a "period certain").

2. Who should consider buying annuities?

Insurance companies will issue (sell) annuities to any adult. Tax-deferred annuities generally work best for people who are in the later stages of the asset accumulation phase (over age 45). Income annuities work best for people over age 60 who have moved into the preservation/income phase and want to plan for the rest of their lives. Annuities don't work well as short-term financial solutions.

3. Is the choice of an insurance company important?

Absolutely. Annuities should only be bought from solid companies that have high ratings. (I'll discuss ratings more in Chapter 21.) In the case of income annuities, it's important to select a company capable of honoring its guarantees over a potentially long time — namely, the rest of your life.

4. Is an annuity the best way to receive an "income you can't outlive"?

It is really the only way to receive a guaranteed and predictable income that you can't outlive. To illustrate why, compare an immediate annuity to two other sources of lifetime income — a pension and Social Security. To many retirees, pensions look like a sure thing for life. We've seen too many examples of pension plans that have failed to meet their obligations financially. When this happens, plans and their obligations may be taken over by a quasi-government agency known as the Pension Benefit Guaranty Corp (PBGC). The PBGC has a good track record for honoring pension payouts to retirees, but PBGC payouts may be capped or revised, compared to the plan's original promises to retirees.

Social Security is a different story, because the issue is not whether you will receive payouts for life but rather how much you might receive in the future, when Social Security runs into financial trouble (see Chapter 14). A guaranteed income from a high-quality life insurance company is backed by the company's assets, protected by state regulations and, ultimately, supported by the reserve funds that most states have set up to protect contract holders. In my opinion, an immediate annuity from a quality insurance company represents a stronger promise to pay guaranteed lifetime income than most pensions or Social Security can make to retirees.

5. Isn't an annuity income vulnerable to inflation?

In a few immediate annuity contracts, it is possible to select an automatic increase in future income payouts to help offset inflation and preserve purchasing power. Another choice, which I don't usually recommend, is called "variable annuitization." It offers the potential for future increases (or decreases) in payout based on the performance of assets linked to the annuity. In this case, the payout level is not predictable or guaranteed. (You can read more on variable annuitization later in this chapter.)

Future inflation should be a concern for all seniors. So, I firmly believe that any plan that includes a fixed annuity payout should also include strategies for maintaining purchasing power, especially if inflation increases. These techniques, which can't always be addressed in the annuity itself, are discussed in Chapters 19 and 23.

The next two chapters will help you understand nuances of the two major types of annuities: 1) tax-deferred annuities for the asset accumulation phase; and 2) income or immediate annuities for your preservation/income phase.

Chapter 16

•••••••••••••

Tax-Deferred Annuities:
Look Closely and Compare

In trying to figure out why the media is generally negative about tax-deferred annuities, I've defined three basic reasons. You can see these reasons at work in the two excerpts below, from two different, well-known magazines:

From *Money* magazine, January 25, 2002: "Are annuities a good bet? They might not be for older investors because you need time to make the investment worthwhile. Also, to overcome high costs and commissions you may have to leave earnings in an annuity for at least a decade."

From *Fortune* magazine, February 7, 2000: "The fundamental problem with annuities of either kind is that you can get them only from insurance companies. In the overwhelming number of cases, the insurers' high cost structure and Dark Ages notions of disclosure and fair play completely undercut the investments' built-in advantages...Variable annuities, for example, charge investors an explicit percentage of assets, as mutual funds do. Alas, in most cases these fees are so high they make variable annuities a losing proposition."

In a nutshell, the media's three main complaints about tax-deferred (accumulation) annuities are:

1. Too complex

2. Takes too long to realize benefits

3. Costs too much

In this chapter, I'll help you look closer at each of these points of criticism. You can make up your own mind about tax-deferred annuities — and that's exactly what I ask each client to do at The Senior Financial

Center. I think these annuities can work, at times, to meet specific needs of clients who understand them and feel comfortable with them. But, if not, alternatives are available.

First, a Story

Donald's story is interesting, because it refutes all three main points of media criticism mentioned above, in a way the media almost never discusses. During his 50s, Donald was asked to leave his company and was offered a cash buyout that left him with approximately $80,000, after income tax. Since Donald was in his accumulation phase and wanted to work at least another 10 years, he decided to invest the money for retirement accumulation, with the hope that the money would eventually pass to his heirs. (He didn't need current income.)

Donald considered three choices for his $80,000: 1) stocks; 2) stock mutual funds; and 3) a "variable" tax-deferred annuity invested in portfolios that are similar to stock mutual funds. After careful consideration, Donald decided on the variable annuity, and he made this choice in the year 1999.

You know what happened next to the stock market. All three choices that Donald considered would have lost almost half his money over the next three years, as the stock market went through its worst bear market since the 1930s. But there was a big difference between the variable annuity and the other two choices, because the annuity included a "guaranteed death benefit." Under this feature, if Donald died, his beneficiary was guaranteed to receive no less than the amount Donald originally invested, $80,000. Thanks to the guaranteed death benefit, Donald didn't feel so badly about his huge market losses. He reasoned: "I may or may not die in the next 10 years. The stock market may or may not come back to where it was in 1999. Whatever happens, as long as I hold this annuity, my heirs won't lose a dime of my original principal at my death."

Here's the part the media doesn't seem to get: The guaranteed death benefit provided valuable protection for Donald and his heirs, but it wasn't free. It is a feature that comes with a cost, called a "mortality and expense (M&E) charge." If you understand the guaranteed death benefit and its cost, tax-deferred variable annuities aren't so complex. If you really want this protection, the whole annuity becomes a better value, and it doesn't take decades for the benefits to be realized (especially in a bear market).

If our clients are in the accumulation phase, want tax-advantaged asset accumulation potential and place a value on the guaranteed death benefit (which apply to variable annuities only), only then do we want to help them evaluate the rest of this solution, starting with the most conservative type — fixed annuities.

Fixed Annuities

A tax-deferred, fixed annuity is a very different story compared to a variable annuity, such as the one Donald held. I believe fixed annuities can have many advantages for clients who are in the accumulation phase, depending on current interest rates and clients' objectives, so let's delve into the details of how they work.

- Most fixed annuities work like short-term CDs, except that the issuer is an insurance company instead of a bank. Your principal and the interest rate are guaranteed by an insurance company instead of by a bank and FDIC insurance. (Fixed annuities are never FDIC-insured, even if they are sold by banks.)

- You deposit money into the fixed annuity in either a lump sum or series of payments. Your money earns a rate of interest guaranteed for a period of time — usually one, two or three years. (It can be longer.)

- Interest is automatically reinvested back into the contract and compounds on a tax-deferred basis. You pay no tax (and don't even report the interest) until withdrawals are taken.

- Assuming that the annuity is not part of a retirement plan, withdrawals are taxed as ordinary income. In addition, a 10% federal tax penalty usually applies on withdrawals taken before age 59½. This penalty is designed to discourage young folks from using fixed annuities as short-term savings havens.

- The fixed annuity contract may impose a "withdrawal charge" on any withdrawals made in the early years, above a given amount. This charge often lasts for 5–8 years and declines annually. It is expressed as a percentage of the amount withdrawn. One common "withdrawal charge schedule" is shown below.

Contract Year	Withdrawal Charge
1	6%
2	5%
3	4%
4	3%
5	2%
6	1%
7	0%

Under this schedule, suppose that you made a withdrawal of $10,000 in the 4th contract year and all of the withdrawal is subject to a withdrawal charge. The applicable percentage is 3%, so the charge would be $300. (This is in addition to federal income tax and the 10% federal penalty, if applicable.)

Note: There are fixed annuities that impose no withdrawal charge. It sounds too good to be true, so be careful. You may receive a lower interest rate in such contracts than in those with withdrawal charges.

- The contract may contain a "free-out" privilege that allows one charge-free withdrawal per year up to a given percent of contract value — often 10%. For example, suppose that the $10,000 withdrawal made in the 4th year (above) has a 10% free-out. Also, assume that the contract value at the time of the withdrawal is $30,000. The first $3,000 withdrawn (10% of contract value) is taken charge-free. The remaining $7,000 is exposed to the 3% charge, so the withdrawal charge would be $210.

- Most fixed annuities allow you to "annuitize" at any time without a withdrawal charge. At "annuitization," you convert the current value of your fixed annuity into a stream of guaranteed payments. The decision to annuitize usually is final and all you are entitled to afterward is the payment stream, not a lump-sum amount. There normally is no tax consequence at the time of annuitization, provided you choose a payout method that lasts at least five years or until you turn age 59½, whichever period is longer. (A portion of each annuitized payment is taxable.)

- Annuitization is rarely ever required in a fixed annuity. It's your choice. Also, there is no requirement to withdraw a minimum amount at older ages, as in Traditional IRAs.

- If you die holding a fixed annuity that has not yet been annuitized, the amount will pass directly to your beneficiary (named in the contract), **bypassing probate**. The value of annuities held in your name normally is included in your taxable estate, and either your estate or the beneficiary will pay any income taxes due on annuity earnings. In annuities held outside retirement plans, your payments into the contract are returned tax free.

Two Questions About Fixed Annuities

Let me answer (before you ask them) two of the most common fixed annuity questions that I hear from senior clients:

1. **Are fixed annuities better than CDs?**

2. **How do I get out of a fixed annuity, assuming I don't annuitize?** (This question is often asked by people who think interest rates will rise. They want to know how they can get money out of a low-rate annuity and put it into something paying higher rates.)

Are Fixed Annuities Better Than CDs?

If you are looking for a place to park your money for the next year or so, don't look at fixed annuities. You'll get very little benefit out of the annuity's tax-deferred compounding over a short period and you may face a hefty surrender charge.

If you won't need to touch this money over several years and want to watch it accumulate with a guarantee as to principal and interest, I think fixed annuities can have four basic advantages over CDs.

1. **No limit on the protection.** CDs are protected by FDIC insurance only up to the FDIC limit ($100,000). In fixed annuities, the insurance company guarantee applies to every dollar.

2. **Tax-deferred compounding.** Given the same interest rate, the fixed annuity will accumulate to a greater value over time because interest is not currently taxable, as in a CD. The longer you hold the annuity, the more valuable tax-deferred compounding will be. You can use the "Rule of 72" to determine how long it will take your money to double in a tax-deferred fixed annuity, assuming no withdrawals. Divide 72 by the estimated interest rate you expect to earn. The result is the number of years it will take your money to double with tax-deferred compounding. Or, you can use the table below.

Interest Rate	Years to Double Money
3.5%	20.6
4.0%	18.0
4.5%	16.0
5.0%	14.4
5.5%	13.1
6.0%	12.0
6.5%	11.1
7.0%	10.3
7.5%	9.6

3. **Higher rates.** At The Senior Financial Center, we specialize in helping seniors shop for the best annuity rates available from quality life insurance companies (in both tax-deferred and immediate annuities). We often find that guaranteed rates in fixed annuities are higher than CD rates with comparable maturities. It pays to shop around!

4. **Free-out privilege.** If you break a CD before maturity, you generally pay a withdrawal charge on every dollar. In a fixed annuity, the free-out allows you to take out a portion of your money once per year without penalty.

How Do I Get Out of a Fixed Annuity If I Don't Annuitize?

A common fixed annuity structure guarantees an interest rate for one or two years, and the withdrawal charge usually lasts several years longer. For example, suppose that you buy a fixed annuity that guarantees a 4.5% interest rate for one year and has a withdrawal charge period of six years. At the end of each year after the first, the insurance company will offer you a "renewal rate" if you keep your money in the contract. Let's say that the renewal rate offered at the end of the first year is still 4.5% but interest rates generally have been rising, and you think that you can do better than 4.5% elsewhere. What choices do you have to take money out, instead of accepting the 4.5% renewal rate?

If you are over age 59½, two choices may make sense.

1. You can take a full withdrawal, pay the charge that applies (on withdrawals in excess of the free-out), and move money to the higher rate. Usually, when this happens in the first year or two, the withdrawal charge eats up most or all of the interest earned. (In some contracts, the withdrawal charge is guaranteed not to eat into principal.)

2. You can withdraw up to the free-out amount each year and move that money elsewhere, while keeping the balance in the fixed annuity. In that case, you don't pay a withdrawal charge.

Suppose you are under age 59 ½ and you have held your fixed annuity through the end of the withdrawal charge period. Now, you want to move the money and receive a higher rate, and your concern is federal income taxes and the 10% penalty, not the contract withdrawal charge. You may wish to take advantage of a little-known technique called a Section 1035 exchange, which allows you to exchange one annuity contract directly for another (without receiving cash) and with no current federal tax consequences. Since a Section 1035 exchange can be a bit technical, make sure you have a qualified professional handle the details for you.

I'd like to sum up my feelings about fixed annuities with the story of Shelly, who inherited a large amount of money right after she retired at age 66 with a full pension, Social Security and a tidy sum in IRAs.

Shelly knew she would have to start taking minimum distributions from her IRA at age 70½, and she didn't want or need any current income from her inheritance. Her goal was to preserve assets while reducing income taxes and increasing her money for old age.

Shelly didn't like the idea of wondering what interest rate the bank would offer each time she rolled over CDs. So, she was a prime candidate for a type of fixed annuity with a long-term interest rate guarantee. She locked up $100,000 in a fixed annuity with a five-year interest rate guarantee at 4.65% per year compounded. Shelly had the peace of mind that her $100,000 would accumulate over five years to $125,515. In this particular fixed annuity, there was no withdrawal charge at the end of five years. So, she could exchange tax free at the end of five years to another annuity (perhaps one offering a higher rate) without charge.

In addition to these benefits, the fixed annuity saved Shelly thousands of dollars in income taxes on her Social Security benefits, compared to currently taxable alternatives such as CDs or bonds. Since fixed annuities don't produce currently taxable income, they don't increase the amount of Social Security that is taxable.

Shelly's case was one in which fixed annuities met her needs better than any alternative. If you, too, want to preserve and accumulate assets, with every dollar guaranteed and without current income tax or Social Security tax consequences, give fixed annuities a close look.

Variable Annuities

Like fixed annuities, variable annuities are tax-deferred solutions designed for long-term accumulation. The difference is that your principal isn't guaranteed in a variable annuity and neither is the rate you earn. Instead, the annuity's value fluctuates up or down with the performance of portfolios that you select. These portfolios are diversified and professionally managed, like mutual funds. Variable annuities are a lot like investing in mutual funds within a tax-advantaged structure.

This is the type of annuity that has incurred most of the media's wrath and you may be wondering why. After all, the media seems to like mutual funds — and variable annuities are just mutual fund look-alikes with extra tax advantages. Go figure.

The answer, in part, probably has to do with the fact that variable annuities impose extra costs above those of mutual funds, including the M&E charge mentioned previously. But, as we have indicated, in return for paying that extra charge, the owner receives a "guaranteed death benefit" that can help to protect heirs against principal loss. I am not a huge advocate of variable annuities, and my reservations about them are not related mainlyto costs. Instead, I've found that most seniors don't really understand what they're buying in a variable annuity. For example, the death benefit doesn't guarantee to pay anything unless the owner holds the contract at death. If your needs change later in life and you cancel the contract, you won't get any protection from the guaranteed death benefit.

There is a way to maintain death benefit protection while lowering your risk with age. That is to select a variable annuity that offers a guaranteed "fixed account" in addition to the mutual fund-like investment portfolios. The fixed account in a variable annuity works exactly like a fixed annuity, and you usually don't pay that extra M&E charge on fixed account assets. Let's say that you put $100,000 into a variable annuity and then lose $20,000 of it. At that point, you are a little older and wiser and your risk tolerance is lower. So, you decide you don't want to lose any more. You can transfer the full amount left over to the fixed account, where principal is protected by an insurance company guarantee. You can't lose any more. But if you die without canceling the contract (or taking any withdrawals), your beneficiary would still receive the $100,000 from the guaranteed death benefit.

For seniors who insist on owning taxable mutual funds and moving money among them periodically, variable annuities can be a better option. Each move between taxable mutual funds generates capital gains or losses. But in a variable annuity, you can shift money among port-folios with no current tax consequence. If you insist on playing the market in retirement and are in a high tax bracket, variable annuities might be worth a look — for part of your nest egg.

Equity Index Annuities

A type of annuity that has grown rapidly in recent years is called an equity index annuity. This, technically, is a fixed annuity, not a security (like a variable annuity). But it also offers stock market participation.

The equity index annuity contract guarantees a minimum return — such as 2.5% on 90% of the deposit. That's the same as a guaranteed return of 2.25% per year, along with a guarantee that 100% of the principal will be returned. In addition, it gives the holder 75–100% of the upside (appreciation) in a specified stock index, usually the Standard & Poor's 500 Index. If the index goes up 12% in a year and the contract participates at 75%, then the return for that year would be 9%. Some contracts limit the upside participation, however, to the 10–12% range. If the index goes up more than that, you don't participate above the limit.

Interest is credited to the contract based on three structures: Annual Rachet, Point to Point and High Water Mark.

- **Annual Rachet** credits increases each year while decreases are ignored. With ratcheting, prior gains from the index cannot be lost due to poor index performance in the future. This structure is most favorable to the consumer.

- **Point-to-Point** uses the high point of the index to determine the growth in annuity value. This approach examines the index at the end of each anniversary and uses the highest index value to determine growth. This is considered the next most favorable.

- **High Water Mark** simply compares beginning and ending index values for the current term. Since the index value could be down at the end of the term measured, this is considered least favorable.

For senior clients who want some stock market participation (and inflation hedge potential) along with a guaranteed return of principal, equity index annuities can make more sense than variable annuities. The guarantees in equity index annuities work to protect capital during your lifetime. You can walk away and be protected against loss. In variable annuities, you are protected against loss only if you are carried away.

Chapter 17

•••••••••••••

Your Odds of Outlasting The Averages

*Note:In this chapter, we'll take a break from our evaluation of an-
nuities to discuss issues relating to your longevity. I think you'll see the
logic of this sequence in the next chapter, which evaluates immediate
annuities and the value of having a guaranteed lifetime income.*

According to an adage that we've all heard and most people
believe: "Everybody wants to go to heaven, but nobody wants to die."

If that's true (and it seems to be), then it's good news that people
are living longer today than ever before. It's also good news that during
the past century, longevity has increased at a rate that is unprecedented
in history. For your great great grandparents, life expectancy was barely
above the ages at which people now tend to retire (see graph below).

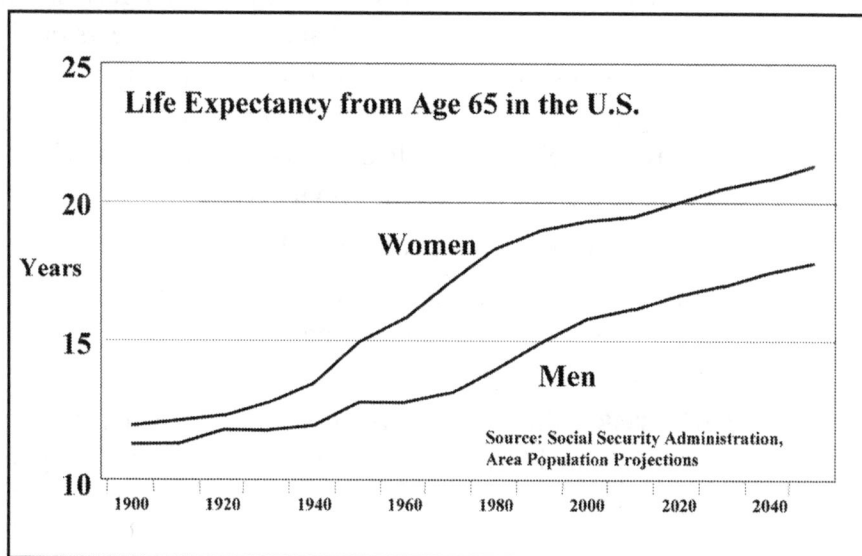

Life Expectancy from Age 65 in the U.S.

Source: Social Security Administration,
Area Population Projections

Today, according to mortality statistics, the **average** woman in the U.S. can expect to live to about age 84. The **average** man in the U.S. can expect to live to approximately age 78. For a married couple, both age 65, the odds that at least one of the two will survive to age 90 are 50-50.

Who wants to be average? Your life expectancy could be even longer than these statistics for a variety of reasons, including heredity, health, exercise, diet and stress. Remember, the averages that I quoted above include people who: 1) have smoked cigarettes for decades; 2) have serious medical conditions; 3) are overweight or don't exercise at all; and 4) work in high-stress jobs or take high risks (including not wearing seat belts in vehicles).

Mortality vs. Longevity Risk

At The Senior Financial Center, we take a great interest in the lifestyles and values of our clients. Based on direct experience, we can point to many clients with an excellent chance of outliving the averages for years because of their histories, healthy habits and positive outlooks on life. When a 75-year-old person returns from a vacation and talks about climbing Machu Picchu, it's a clue that longevity planning is an important issue!

Here's why I take these clues seriously. When you really get to know seniors as their financial advisor, you learn that their biggest fears rarely have to do with next month or next year. Instead, many seniors worry about having enough money to deal with their last years. To convince clients that they have enough money to live worry-free for the rest of their lives, we need to have a sense of their "longevity risk."

"Longevity risk" is the opposite of "mortality risk."

- **Mortality risk** is a responsibility to provide financial security if a person dies soon. The longer a person may live, the lower mortality risk is.

- **Longevity risk** is the responsibility to provide financial security if a person lives too long. The longer a person may live, the higher longevity risk is.

As you will learn in the next chapter, life insurance companies assess and assume longevity risk, in addition to mortality risk.

- They assume **mortality risk** in issuing **life insurance** policies.
- They assume **longevity risk** in issuing **immediate (income) annuities**.

Here's a big and important difference. Suppose that you have been diagnosed with severe hypertension or congestive heart failure and you apply for life insurance. What is virtually guaranteed to happen? Most likely, your application will be declined because, based on medical underwriting, you represent a greater mortality risk than the insurance company can afford. Even if you find a company that will accept you, it will be at a huge "rated" premium that compensates for your high mortality risk.

On the other side of the coin, longevity risk, insurance companies are not allowed to underwrite. They can't reject you because you're in great health, walk two miles a day, have never smoked and have parents who lived to age 100. The law doesn't allow it. Even if it's obvious that you probably will live a long time, insurance companies that issue income annuities can't decline you or charge you more.

This is why we help clients assess their longevity risk and then, if it is above average, help them take advantage of a great deal — the opportunity to lay off this risk on an insurance company on the same terms as people of the same age and sex with lower longevity risk.

Assessing Your Longevity Risk

At the end of this chapter is a worksheet called *Will You Live Longer Than an Average Lifespan?* The 12 questions on this worksheet will help you determine whether you can expect to live longer than average.

Why is it important to know your longevity risk?

If you are retired or planning ahead for retirement, one of your goals may be to avoid outliving your assets. The longer you expect to live, the more challenging this goal may be. That's especially true if you depend largely on savings and investments for current income, because inflation gradually reduces the purchasing power of a fixed income over time.

For example, if you stand a good chance of living more than approximatey 20 years, you can apply the Rule of 5% to see that without longevity protection your assets will be nearly exhausted during your lifetime. The Rule of 5% says this:

- If you earn a 5% annual return on your assets, after tax; and
- Inflation averages 5% per year for the rest of your life; and
- You withdraw 5% of your nest egg in the first year and increase the withdrawal in each subsequent year by 5% to offset inflation, then…

Your nest egg will be depleted just after the 20th year. The Rule of 5% works whether your nest egg is $10,000 or $1 million. The graph below shows how a $1 million nest egg would be depleted under the Rule of 5% at a point in the 20th year.

The Rule of 5%: An Example

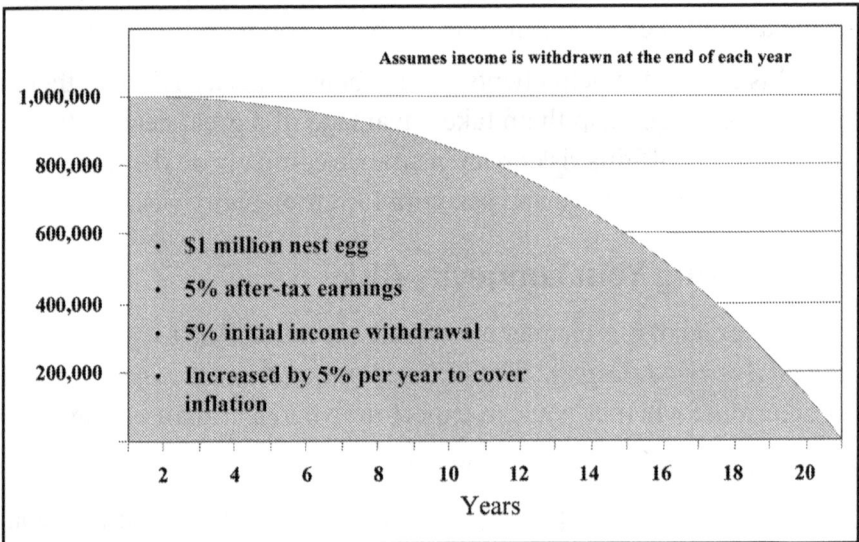

Assumes income is withdrawn at the end of each year

- $1 million nest egg
- 5% after-tax earnings
- 5% initial income withdrawal
- Increased by 5% per year to cover inflation

Years

In the past, Social Security has been a source of lifetime income upon which many retired people have relied. However, the longer you live, the less likely it may be that you can count on Social Security for a large part of retirement security. As you may know, Social Security will strain to meet current obligations as massive amounts of Baby Boomers retire (see Chapter 14). While Social Security benefits appear solid now (and in the near future), they may become more iffy if you live a long time. That's why it's even more important to make sound decisions that can help you stretch savings longer.

Four Steps to Financial Security

To address the challenge of assessing and planning for personal longevity risk, I urge you to do four things:

1. Complete the worksheet at the end of this chapter to assess your personal longevity risk.

2. Determine how much longevity risk you want to lay off on an insurance company. (In the next chapter I'll tell you how.)

3. Create a strategy that will help to protect your assets against inflation.

4. Review your "longevity plan" periodically, perhaps annually, to make sure that you are on track to make your assets last as long as you do, even if you last a very long time.

In a nutshell, real retirement planning begins with the security of knowing that your assets will last through your last year, whenever that may be. You don't want to achieve that sense of security "at long last." You need it now, and in my humble opinion, you deserve it now!

Will You Live Longer Than an Average Lifespan?

Circle the answer that applies. Check your score using the "Longevity Key."

#	Question	Col. A	Col. B	Col. C
1.	Which of your parents lived to age 70 (or probably will)?	Both	One	None
2.	How many incidents of cardiovascular problems has your family experienced?	None	One	More than one
3.	How often do you exercise vigorously?	Regularly	Occasionally	Almost never
4.	How is your blood pressure?	Low or normal	A little high	Very high
5.	Have you ever suffered a serious illness involving heart, liver, kidneys, lungs or other major	No	Once, minor	More than once or major
6.	Are you a smoker?	No	Light	Heavy
7.	Are you a drinker?	No	Modest	Heavy
8.	How's your weight in proportion to your height?	Average or below	A little high	Quite high
9.	How stressful is (was) your line of work?	Not at all	Modest	Very
10.	How would you describe your diet?	All the right stuff	I try but snack	All the wrong stuff
11.	What protects you when you drive?	Seat belt and air bags	Seat belt or air bag, but not both	Nothing between me & the windshield
12.	How is the air quality where you live?	Great	Average	Poor
Total answers in each column:				
Multiply totals		x 2	x 1	
Total Points				
Add Total Points in Columns A and B. This is your Longevity Score.				

If your Longevity Score is...	You might reasonably expect...
20–24	•To live at least 6–10 years beyond normal life expectancy
15–19	•To live 1–5 years beyond normal life expectancy
8–14	•To live about average life expectancy
Less than 8	•To live less than average life expectancy

Chapter 18

•••••••••••••

Immediate Annuities and Annuitization: Locking It in for Life

Immediate annuities help you manage the longevity dilemma by transferring risk to a life insurance company, without any underwriting of your health. These annuities are purchased with a one-time (lump-sum) payment, or else by "annuitizing" a tax-deferred annuity balance. The transaction converts an asset into a stream of guaranteed income payments, and the buyer usually gives up all rights to principal.

Immediate annuities offer several benefits to seniors who are in the asset preservation/income stage and wish to maximize current income.

- The immediate annuity market is very competitive. With the help of a financial advisor, you can compare quotes from many high-quality companies.

- You can choose an income payout frequency (e.g., monthly, quarterly or annually) that suits you.

- You can choose an income payout that will last over your own life, two lives, or a specific period of time.

- Once you have chosen a payout frequency and method, the amount of guaranteed income you will receive usually is predictable and level. (It also can be variable, under one type of annuity.)

- If you are purchasing the annuity with non-retirement plan money (or annuitizing a non-retirement plan tax-deferred annuity), the tax treatment of each payment is favorable.

- You don't necessarily have to disenfranchise your heirs by selecting an immediate annuity. In the next chapter, I'll discuss a technique we often use to maximize current income while also preserving assets for heirs and reducing estate taxes.

A One-Time Choice

Before explaining more about immediate annuities, let me address the most common (and serious) questions clients ask about this strategy:

1. What if I make this choice and then want to change my mind?

2. Aren't these fixed payments vulnerable to inflation, and won't my purchasing power gradually be reduced over time?

The answer to the first question should be obvious if you think carefully about the idea of laying off longevity risk on a life insurance company. Suppose that two months after you purchase an immediate annuity, you suffer a heart attack or stroke. Your personal life expectancy would decline by many years. At that point, if you could call up the life insurance company, cancel your contract and get your money back, it would be a great deal for you. It also would be a terrible deal for the life insurance company. Eventually, if everybody did that, the only people left owning immediate annuities would be a few 100-year-olds in perfect health, and insurance companies could go broke. The tradeoff in laying off longevity risk is that it is a one-time decision and the consequences are permanent. That's why it's such an important decision that should only be made after reviewing your goals with a qualified advisor.

The answer to the last question shouldn't affect your decision as to **whether** to lay off longevity risk. It can determine how much money you put toward this goal, compared to others, or how you apply annuity income to other goals. In the next chapter, I'll discuss a few ways to combine immediate annuities with other strategies to protect your purchasing power against inflation.

The key point in answering these questions is this: Don't ever make the important decision to purchase an immediate annuity (or annuitize a tax-deferred annuity) in a vacuum. The decision and related choices should always be made in the context of your total retirement and estate planning needs. For married people, I prefer to have both spouses involved in this planning and final agreement. It also can help, in some cases, to involve other family members.

Shopping for an Immediate Annuity

Suppose that you are a 70-year-old female, married to a 70-year-old male and have $100,000 to put toward an immediate annuity. If you "went shopping" for an immediate annuity, the table below shows some choices you might find. (The income payouts or "rates" quoted below are hypothetical. Insurance companies change their immediate annuity rates all the time. The "annuitant" is the person, or people, to whom payments are made.)

Payout Choice	What It Means	Sample Monthly Income Quote
Single Life	Income will be paid for the rest of your life with no payout after your death to your beneficiary.	**$665**
Single Life with 10 Years Period Certain (PC)	Income will be paid for the rest of your life. If you die within 10 years, the same payments will continue to your beneficiary until the end of the 10th year.	**$644**
Single Life with 20 Years PC	Ditto the above, except that payments will continue to your beneficiary until the end of the 20th year.	**$579**
Joint & 100% Survivor	Full payments will continue until the last of two annuitants dies.	**$592**
Joint & 100% Survivor with 20 Years PC	Ditto the above, except that payments will continue to your beneficiary until the end of the 20th year.	**$558**
Joint & 50% Survivor	Full payments will continue until the death of the first annuitant. Half payments will then be made until the death of the second annuitant.	**$612**
20 Years PC	Payments will be made for a fixed period of 20 years.	**$591**

Even if you are the world's greatest shopper, you probably find these choices confusing. So, how should you proceed to make the best decision?

Five Questions to Help You Shop

The table below contains five questions that I think are critical.

	Yes	Maybe	No
1. Do you think you might live longer than your average life expectancy?	____	____	____
2. Do you want to lay off some longevity risk on a life insurance company?	____	____	____
3. Do you want to provide (from this source) financial security for a spouse after your death?	____	____	____
4. Do you want to provide (from this source) money for heirs after your death?	____	____	____
5. Would you prefer to provide security for a spouse and money for heirs from a different source than this?	____	____	____

Analysis of your answers:

- If you answered "yes" to either (or both) questions 1 and 2, you should choose a single life or joint & survivor payout. There is no "longevity risk transfer" in a PC payout.
- If you answered "yes" to question 3, you may want to choose a joint & survivor payout method. Answering this question "maybe" may point toward a joint & 50% survivor choice. Or it could mean you need to evaluate this choice in more depth.
- If you answered "yes" to question 4, you may want to add a PC to a lifetime (or joint & survivor) payout.

- If you answered "yes" to question 5, the best choice may be to leverage your own longevity by choosing a straight single life payout (with no PC). You then have the option of applying part of the extra annuity income to other financial goals.

I believe these five questions are best addressed within a comprehensive planning process guided by a qualified financial advisor. If you come to The Senior Financial Center to evaluate immediate annuity choices, we'll work through the process with you.

Living on Your Annuity Income

In evaluating immediate annuities, it's important to understand that the income itself can be planned to meet a variety of goals. For example, earlier in this chapter we illustrated hypothetical income quotes available to a 70-year-old woman, including the following (per $100,000):

- Single Life $665 per month
- Single Life with 20 Years PC $579 per month

This woman wants to leave her children and grandchildren something when she dies. So, she feels inclined to take the choice with a 20 years PC. That way, if she dies in (let's say) the 15th year, her heirs would still get five more years of guaranteed payments.

There is another way to remember heirs that could offer even more flexibility down the road. Suppose she "maxes out" her income by taking the single life payout and then "saves the difference" into a flexible premium fixed annuity (tax-deferred) paying 5%. The difference in the two payouts above is $86 per month per $100,000. (**Note:** "Flexible premium" means you can keep adding small amounts to the annuity.)

Over 15 years, saving $86 per month at a 5% compound rate, tax-deferred, would accumulate to a hypothetical $23,083. So, she wouldn't be leaving her heirs with nothing, if she died after 15 years. They could get $23,083 (per $100,000) by inheriting her fixed annuity. If she wanted to leave them even more, she might consider adding a modest amount of life insurance to this plan.

Of course, her heirs would have to pay tax on the fixed annuity earnings at her death, so they would receive something less than $23,083 after tax. As an alternative, there may be an even better option for turning that $86 per month into a meaningful legacy for heirs, after taxes are considered. I'll get to that strategy in the next chapter.

The point of this example is that the "income max" choice does have advantages, because it creates more income along with more flexibility, compared to other options. For example, suppose that inflation goes higher and this annuitant needs more income to maintain her purchasing power. In that case, she could stop saving $86 per month in the fixed annuity and apply it to her own needs. Or, she might choose to use it to make lifetime gifts to her heirs (such as helping to put a grandchild through college). Just remember that the single life payout = max income = more flexibility.

Taxes on Annuity Payouts

Note: The information in this section relates to annuity payments **not** made in retirement plans. For information on retirement plan annuity payouts, including IRAs, refer to the next section.

A "hidden benefit"of annuity payouts is the favorable tax treatment that they receive from the IRS compared to other sources of current income, especially CDs. If you put $100,000 into a CD and can earn 4%, you will receive an annual income of $4,000, of which 100% is included in your taxable income. But if you receive $4,000 from an immediate annuity (not paid out inside a retirement plan), only a small portion of payments are taxable. The rest is considered a non-taxable return of your principal. This can be a valuable benefit in reducing your regular income taxes and the tax on your Social Security.

At the time you annuitize, the company that you choose will determine an "exclusion ratio" using an IRS formula. It takes into account:

1. The amount of premium you pay to buy the annuity or the value of the tax-deferred annuity that you annuitize. This is the numerator (top number) in a fraction.

2. The total number of payments you can expect to receive, given the payout method you select and your life expectancy, and the amount of each payment. This is the denominator (bottom number) in a fraction.

Example: You pay $100,000 to buy an immediate annuity. The insurance company calculates that you can expect to receive 18 years' worth of monthly payments (216 payments in total) worth $575 each. The total of all payments is $124,200 (216 x $575). The fraction is as follows:

Annuity Premium	$100,000	= 80.5% exclusion ratio
Total Payments Expected	$124,200	

Your exclusion ratio will remain at 80.5% for 18 years. On each of the first 216 payments, 80.5% will be a non-taxable return of principal and only 19.5% will be taxable.

- You will include as taxable income $112 per payment or $1,344 per year.
- You will not pay any tax on $463 per payment or $5,554 per year.

If you continue to collect any payments after the 18th year, you would have then received back all of your principal (for tax purposes) and 100% of each payment would be taxable income.

Some seniors don't think they are in a high enough tax bracket for income taxes to matter much. But, in some cases, that's far from the truth.

- If an extra dollar of taxable income is taxed at a 15% federal income tax rate, and also subjects 50% of Social Security benefits to tax (because it pushes you over the thresholds discussed in Chapter 14), then the effective federal rate on that income is 22.5%. With state income taxes added, the rate could go higher than 25%.
- If an extra dollar of taxable income is taxed at a 25% federal income tax rate, and also subjects 85% of Social Security benefits to tax, then the effective federal rate on that income could be

33.75%. With state income taxes added, the rate could go higher than 40%.

Choosing an immediate annuity can be an effective way to permanently manage and reduce income taxes for the rest of your life — or at least as long as your annuity payments are expected to last at the time of purchase.

As a small but meaningful side benefit, you don't have to calculate the exclusion ratio or taxable portion of payments yourself. It's done for you by the life insurance company and reported to the IRS (with a statement sent to you).

For more information on the reporting or taxation on non-qualified annuity payments, you can refer to *IRS Publication 590.*

Qualified Immediate Annuities

Many seniors who own IRAs dread the approach of one "birthday," which only the IRS celebrates. That is your 70½ birthday.

Why does the IRS celebrate? Your 70 ½ birthday marks the point at which you must soon start taking annual required distributions from IRAs (and also company retirement plans). For details on how minimum distributions are calculated, see Chapter 9.

Many seniors don't know that they have an option that will avoid the need to ever make these calculations. That choice is to annuitize IRA money into guaranteed payments over a period not greater than life expectancy. All payments made from such annuities are fully taxable, just as the required minimum distributions would be. Annuities that are designed to hold retirement plan money (or pay out guaranteed income from this money) are called "qualified annuities."

I look at annuitization of IRAs as a "peace-of-mind solution" to minimum distribution requirements, with the added benefit of transferring longevity risk to an insurance company. You also may have the option of annuitizing any amounts you still have in a defined contribution retirement plan at work, such as a 401(k). For starters, you can check and see if your plan offers an annuity payout option. If not, don't despair. In my experience, you will expand your annuity choices through a two-step process:

1. First, you directly transfer or roll over your plan money to a Traditional IRA.

2. For the Traditional IRA, you can choose a qualified fixed annuity (and then annuitize at a later time) or a qualified immediate annuity.

Variable Annuitization

One type of immediate annuity (or annuitization choice) offers you a stream of payments that are guaranteed as to the time period (or number of payments), not as to the amounts to be paid out. It is called "variable annuitization." For example, if you take this choice on a Single Life basis, you still are guaranteed to receive payments as long as you live. The amount of payments will rise or fall with the performance of underlying investment portfolios linked to your account.

Advocates of variable annuitization say that it can be a way to protect your purchasing power against inflation, because payments can rise over time with stock market performance. My reply to this idea is that the probability of continued inflation is much greater than the probability that the stock market will keep going up. You could lose a lot of money, along with part of your retirement lifestyle, if your investments don't pan out.

In fact, you could lose a lot even if the market doesn't decline over time. To consider an example, suppose that you had chosen variable annuitization just before the bear market of 2000–2002 and linked your payments to a stock fund. Your income would have taken a severe dip during that period, and even if the market gradually recovered, you would have sacrificed that income permanently.

I think the major reason to select an immediate annuity is peace of mind, combined with the ability to plan your retirement budgets and perhaps generate more current income. With variable annuitization, you can't do that **with certainty**. There will always be worries in the back of your mind. If you want growth potential or inflation-hedging strategies in your retirement plan, it might be best to look for them elsewhere — not in immediate annuities.

Chapter 19

•••••••••••••

The Power of an Asset Preservation Strategy

At The Senior Financial Center, our clients often have the following retirement goals, in approximately this order:

1. Preserve all of my principal and not expose any of it to high risk.

2. Generate more income than I can earn in bank CD interest, with flexibility to participate in any rising interest rate environment and avoid having my income run out in old age.

3. Maintain flexibility to make changes or purchases, if that becomes attractive.

4. Have some money available for heirs at my death.

5. Avoid paying more income or estate taxes than necessary.

6. Avoid probate and any unnecessary fees or delays in transferring assets.

To help clients pursue these goals, we have developed a simple strategy that packs great retirement planning power. We call it our Asset Preservation Strategy. In so many cases, it has lifted loads of risk and worry off our clients' shoulders immediately, so that they can "start living the good life" of retirement right away.

The strategy takes advantage of "planning synergy" that can be achieved when you combine an immediate annuity, a fixed annuity and (in some cases) life insurance. The combination of these solutions, carefully planned, can have more benefit than each delivered separately.

To illustrate, let's discuss the situation of Otis and Lou Ellen, a couple who came to us after selling their business and retiring. They had about $600,000 in liquid assets, most of it in CDs or mutual funds, in addition to their home, a pension and two IRAs. But at that time, CD interest rates were in the 2% to 3% range, and they had already lost a fortune in mutual funds. Despite a lifetime of hard work and the sale of a successful business, they didn't feel wealthy and wondered whether they could even afford to retire. They were in their mid-60s at the time, about ready to start collecting Social Security.

Once they saw the wisdom of our Asset Preservation Strategy, the weight of making so many complex decisions disappeared. They no longer had to worry about shopping for CD rates every year, or whether they should risk one cent in mutual funds. In addition to their goal of generating enough predictable retirement income to maintain their standard of living, they also had two other goals:

1. They were thinking of selling their home in the New York area and moving to a warmer climate, and they thought they might need access to liquid funds for a down payment and transaction costs. Also, they wanted the flexibility to buy Otis' lifelong dream, a power boat.

2. They wanted to leave some assets after the second spouse's death to their children and grandchildren — not a fortune, just enough to say they planned well and cared to remember.

It often takes our staff two or more meetings with clients like Otis and Lou Ellen to create comfort and get these goals "on the table." So, while the Asset Preservation Strategy may seem simple, it can take work and patience to make sure it is the best retirement plan for a given client.

A Two-Bucket Strategy

The Asset Preservation Strategy divides a sum of money into two "buckets":

1. One bucket is for **guaranteed current income**, which is generated by an immediate annuity.

2. The other is for **growth with guaranteed principal protection**, generated by a tax-deferred fixed annuity.

The illustration below shows how we divided Otis and Lou Ellen's $600,000 into these buckets, and the outcome.

1. In the **guaranteed current income bucket**, they could count on receiving an income of $1,805 per month for the next 10 years. In the Asset Preservation Strategy, we use immediate annuities with a period certain payout (e.g. 10 years in this case). Remember that PC annuities **do not** lay off longevity risk on an insurance company. Even if both Otis and Lou Ellen were to die before the end of 10 years, payments would continue to their heirs. Even if they lived well beyond 10 years, payments would stop at the end of 10 years. (Bear with me and I'll explain how this strategy achieves longevity protection.)

    Of the $600,000 they had available, $188,000 was allocated to the guaranteed current income bucket, representing 31.3% of the total. When the guaranteed income of $1,805 was added to their other income sources (Social Security, pension, IRA), we estimated that they would have an annual income of about $45,000 per year in retirement. Only about 20% of each immediate annuity payment would be included in their taxable income. Also, very little (if any) of their Social Security would be subject to income tax. They could indeed afford to start enjoying retirement right away.

2. We allocated the remaining $412,000 of their money to the second bucket, which we will call "asset accumulation with principal protection." In this bucket, we purchased a tax-deferred fixed annuity in which all principal is 100% guaranteed and in which an interest rate is guaranteed for a period. The strategy aims to hold this fixed annuity for the full 10 years, until the immediate annuity income in bucket #1 terminates. However, the interest rate in fixed annuities usually is guaranteed for a shorter income period, perhaps 1–5 years. After the initial interest guaranteed period, the fixed annuity will declare a "renewal rate" that is influenced by current interest rates.

So, we conservatively estimate an average interest rate that might be achieved by the fixed annuity over the full 10 years. In this case, we estimated 3.8%. The single premium deposit to the fixed annuity bucket was $412,000. At a 3.8% tax-deferred compound rate over 10 years, we projected that bucket #2 would grow over 10 years to a sum of $600,000. In other words, they would end the 10 years with exactly the same amount of principal that they had at the beginning. During the whole period, every cent of their principal and income would be guaranteed by quality life insurance companies.

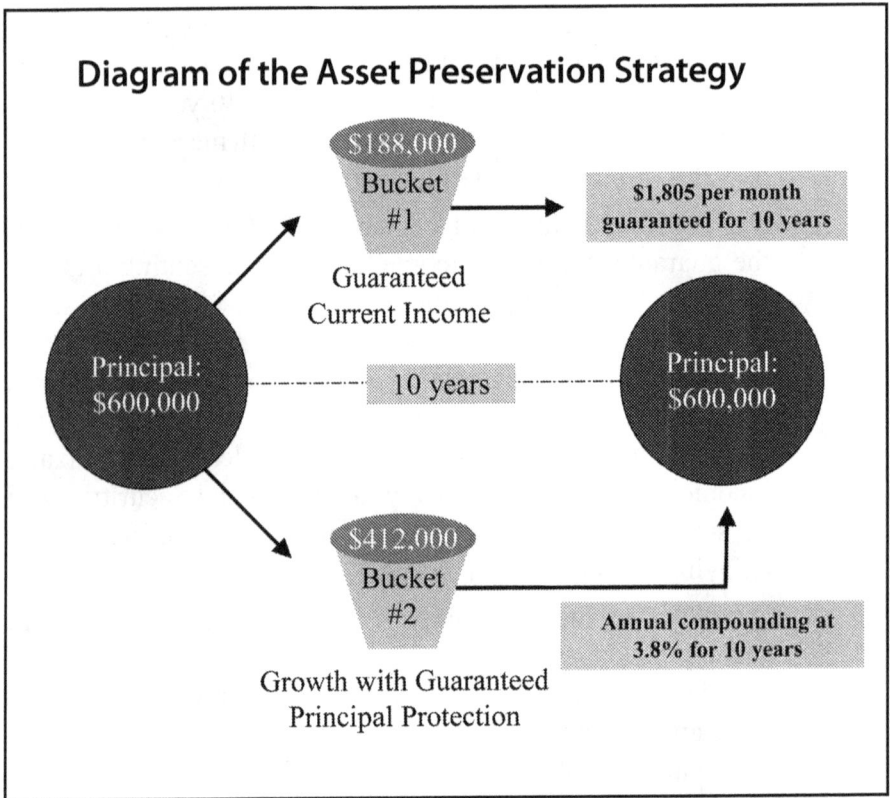

Diagram of the Asset Preservation Strategy

$188,000
Bucket #1

$1,805 per month guaranteed for 10 years

Guaranteed Current Income

Principal: $600,000

10 years

Principal: $600,000

$412,000
Bucket #2

Annual compounding at 3.8% for 10 years

Growth with Guaranteed Principal Protection

Now that you understand the Asset Preservation Strategy, I'll tell you how we decide how much money to allocate to the two buckets. We start with the amount of principal you want to remain intact at the end of the period, and then we work backward. In this example, Otis and Lou Ellen wanted to keep 100% of their principal ($600,000) intact after 10 years. But you might decide that you would be comfortable having only 90% intact. That would result in more money going into the immediate annuity and more current income.

Asset Preservation With Flexibility

How does this strategy address goal #3 in our list mentioned earlier — "maintain flexibility to make major purchases, if that becomes attractive"?"The fixed annuity "free-out" provision offers the ability to tap a sum of money (typically up to 10% of the annuity value) without withdrawal charge, whenever you might want to make a major purchase. Of course, taking a free-out withdrawal would reduce the amount of fixed annuity assets, so that your principal would not stay intact at the end of the period. But you would have the flexibility to make that choice at any time.

What will happen at the end of 10 years? Assuming both spouses are still alive, we will sit down with them again and consider whether it makes sense to repeat the strategy or pursue a different one. If only one spouse survives the 10 years, all of the income payments in the income bucket would continue to the survivor. All of the principal in the asset accumulation bucket would pass to the survivor, the joint owner of the fixed annuity.

Of course, it is possible that many changes could occur over 10 years in Otis and Lou Ellen's goals and health, interest rates and inflation, and other economic conditions. But after 10 years, they would have total flexibility to revise their plan and accommodate changes. They should have virtually all of their principal intact after 10 years, too. So, in effect, they would have the option of renewing their Asset Protection Strategy 10 years deep into retirement. This is how the strategy offers protection against longevity and outliving your assets.

Heirs and Estates

Like most of our clients, Otis and Lou Ellen quickly saw how the Asset Preservation Strategy met the first three goals identified at the start of this chapter, but what about goal #4 (money available for heirs at the second death) and #5 (avoid paying more income or estate tax than necessary)?

Two options embedded in the strategy allow you to plan customized bequests to heirs.

1. You can name heirs (aside from your spouse) as the contingent beneficiaries of both the immediate and fixed annuities. If both spouses were to die, remaining income payments and assets would pass to designated heirs.

2. You could set aside a portion of each annuity income payment as a premium to purchase a second-to-die (survivorship) life insurance policy. The death benefit of this policy could be designated for one or more heirs to meet goal #4. I usually suggest a permanent type of life insurance such as whole life or universal life, because these policies allow premiums to be locked in. (Premiums do not keep increasing with age, as in term life insurance.)

Let's say that Otis and Lou Ellen acquire a survivorship life insurance policy and pay the premiums with part of their annuity income. It has a $100,000 death benefit payable to heirs. Then, suppose that Otis dies after five years and Lou Ellen after 10. Lou Ellen would continue to participate in all benefits of the Asset Preservation Strategy after Otis' death. At Lou Ellen's death, heirs would receive the value of the fixed annuity plus the $100,000 death benefit on the life insurance.

Is this a tax-smart strategy that can also help to achieve goal #5, tax minimization? It is indeed, in several ways:

- As previously mentioned, only approximately 20% of the immediate annuity payments are taxable. (The balance is a non-taxable return of principal.)

- If they decide to renew or "roll over" the strategy at the end of 10 years, they can make a tax-free transfer from the old fixed annuity into new annuities.

- If one spouse dies, there usually is no current income or estate tax consequence to the surviving spouse. Most fixed annuities offer "spousal continuation rights" to a surviving spouse joint owner. Also, unlimited assets may be transferred to a surviving spouse at death without federal estate tax consequences.

- At the death of the second spouse, the fixed annuity balance becomes taxable income and it also can be subject to estate tax.

However, the life insurance will pass income tax-free to heirs and can be used to offset most of the tax on the fixed annuity. With planning techniques described in Chapter 22, the life insurance death benefit also can be received estate tax-free.

Questions About the Strategy

Of course, no retirement planning strategy is so wonderful that it will work for everybody. We do hear some questions or objections about the Asset Preservation Strategy, including:

- It doesn't offer growth potential.
- How will it help me protect my purchasing power against inflation?
- There is no guarantee that the interest rate assumed in the fixed annuity will be achieved over all 10 years.
- Is this really the most tax-efficient way to pass assets to my heirs?

These can be valid issues to consider. We have found that even if the Asset Preservation Strategy doesn't ultimately become the best solution available for a particular client, we like to at least discuss it — because it can make so many inferior planning choices disappear. Once you see that you can afford to retire without excessive risk or worry, without depending on the promises of stockbrokers or the changing CD rates of banks, you will be "in the groove" to make the best decisions for your retirement.

Chapter 20

•••••••••••••

Life Insurance after 60:
When Does It Make Sense?

By the time you get to be age 60 or better, you know a lot more about life insurance than when you were first approached by a life insurance agent — probably when you were in your 20s or early 30s. Specifically, you know:

1. Huge numbers of individuals and institutions want to sell you life insurance, even if you don't think you need it.

2. A primary role of life insurance is to protect your income and the financial security of your dependents. These needs are **not** as important in retirement as when you are raising a family.

3. Seniors have a higher risk of dying than younger people, and so their life insurance coverage costs more.

These points aren't a matter of opinion. They are well-known facts.

It's amazing how often some life insurance agents will dance around these points, not conceding they are true and, in effect, questioning your intelligence and experience. It is much more helpful to begin the discussion where these points leave off.

1. For most seniors, there is no reason to consider life insurance until a specific need for it has been identified in your retirement/estate planning.

2. That need probably will be different than your need for life insurance earlier in life, when you had more dependents under your roof.

3. Life insurance for seniors must make cost-effective sense, by potentially saving you money in areas such as probate court, federal income tax, federal estate tax or long-term care. Unless you can see real "bang for the buck," you may not need life insurance after 60.

In this chapter, we'll discuss several ways that we have developed cost-effective life insurance strategies that focus on specific needs of seniors. In Chapter 21, we'll offer suggestions on choosing life insurance and annuity companies, including ideas on how to compare costs. Chapter 22 covers a potentially valuable technique for passing assets to heirs through life insurance with maximum tax efficiency.

Senior Needs Met by Life Insurance

There are five major types of needs that life insurance can help seniors meet:

1. Leaving assets to heirs on a tax-efficient basis, without going through probate.
2. Planning for and pre-paying estate taxes and settlement costs.
3. Obtaining LTCI protection economically, through an option or rider embedded in some life insurance policies.
4. Arranging the transition of a business to a partner or successor owner.
5. Generating additional retirement income.

Leaving Assets to Heirs

I often engage a client in this type of discussion: "You say that you want to leave some money to your family. But do you also want to leave them taxes to pay?" Usually, the client's answer has two parts:

1. Of course I don't want to leave my heirs tax obligations. Nobody wants to pay taxes.
2. I've never thought about leaving my heirs taxes. How can I avoid it?

Life insurance isn't the only answer, but it is often one of the best. The death benefit in a life insurance contract passes to the beneficiary income tax-free. By using a planning technique discussed in Chapter 23, it also is possible to pass assets to heirs without federal estate tax consequences.

Other important considerations include simplicity, privacy and probate. Typically, after people die, life insurance death benefits are among the first assets released to heirs — often within a few weeks after a death certificate is presented and a claim is filed. Since the executor usually files the death certificate and claim, heirs don't need to do anything to receive their bequests. Unlike many other types of property, life insurance does not pass through probate court and isn't subject to probate's public scrutiny or fees.

Planning for and Pre-Paying Estate Taxes and Settlement Costs

A half century ago, a large part of the life insurance sold in the U.S. was designated for "burial costs." Today, funerals cost far more than they did then — but burial is a small part of the cost in wrapping up affairs of a deceased. As you learned in Chapter 5, estate taxes remain costly and uncertain, despite recent changes in the law. Other costs include state inheritance taxes, payment of the deceased's debts, probate and executor fees, preparation of the deceased's final reports and tax returns, and final tax payments. Life insurance can be useful in planning for and pre-paying these costs.

In my experience, when families start feuding over "who gets what" in an estate, the battles aren't always about assets. Just as often, they are about allocating costs and expenses. Rather than leaving to chance (or politics) which heirs will get stuck with taxes and costs, it can be smart to let life insurance pay the bills.

Arranging the Transition of a Business to a Partner or Successor Owner

It's common to find business owners in their 50s whose goals are to retire in the next 10 or so years. But 15–20 years later, they still haven't let go. Why? They don't know how. Specifically, they can't find a way to extract the market value of the business and turn it into liquid cash. The greatest difficulty and complexity occurs if they die before extracting business value, leaving a surviving spouse or heirs with their grief and an unfamiliar business to run.

Life insurance can be one component in a plan of "business continuity and succession." That usually means phasing out the boss while protecting what the boss has built for the benefit of his/her own retirement as well as family and heirs. The business owner's life is insured and, often, a second policy is purchased on the person chosen as the successor owner or manager. If the owner dies, the death benefit allows either the business itself or the successor owner to buy out the owner's interest, paying heirs the fair market value in cash. If the chosen successor dies, the business is protected and can use the money to pursue other succession strategies.

An agreement called a "buy-sell" is drafted to clarify the rights of the parties in the event of the death (and sometimes the disability) of the other. In some business succession plans, contingencies can be made for transferring the business based on the owner's normal retirement, as well.

Generating Additional Retirement Income

Most people don't think of life insurance as the best source for obtaining retirement income. In fact, life insurance is often used by financial planners to generate supplemental retirement income that "tops off" amounts generated by Social Security, pensions, retirement plans and annuities. Permanent ("cash value") life insurance can be especially useful when:

1. The need for supplemental income is temporary or short-term.

2. The owner is in a high tax bracket.

3. Life insurance is useful in meeting other needs, such as estate planning.

Most policies allow income to be obtained from two sources:

- **Low-cost loans** that are often tax-free and may be repaid at any time.

- **Withdrawals of cash value** that are allowed without withdrawal charge, and are received tax-free (as a return of premium) up to the total amount of premium paid in.

If the cash value of a policy is large enough, it is possible to take a stream of tax-free income from a life insurance policy (as either a loan or withdrawal) for several years, while still maintaining the policy's death benefit protection. In some policies, the death benefit remains level, even if the cash value is depleted via loans or withdrawals.

Tax-advantaged loans and withdrawals are not allowed in "Modified Endowment Contracts," which include single-pay whole life (SPWL) and single-pay universal life (SPUL) insurance contracts.

Look at Life Insurance through Different Eyes

When you were in your 20s, 30s and 40s, life insurance was a critical part of your financial foundation. If you had dependents to feed and shelter, you needed life insurance — whether or not you wanted it.

Once you approach retirement, that is no longer the case. Life insurance is not a necessity — you may want to think of it as a planning option. It can open new possibilities for addressing specific needs in a cost-effective and tax-efficient way. It also can increase your peace of mind, create the income you need to afford special opportunities, keep your heirs from squabbling and help you obtain long-term care economically.

What doesn't change from your 30s through your 60s and beyond is the need to shop wisely for strong life insurance companies offering affordable costs. That is the subject of the next chapter.

Chapter 21

•••••••••••••

Shopping for Life Insurance: Focus on Quality and Cost

I like to divide the decisions involving life insurance into two compartments. If you become our client at The Senior Financial Center, in the first compartment we will work together to decide whether you need life insurance during retirement and, if so, the specific needs it will address. In the second compartment, we'll shop among a variety of insurance companies for a combination of quality and cost.

We all know that seniors are the smartest financial consumers, due to their years of experience combined with an instinctive desire to preserve assets. Even so, I find great confusion among many seniors regarding the issues of life insurance quality and cost. In this chapter, I'll help you answer questions such as:

- What defines an insurance company's quality, for shopping purposes?
- How is a life insurance company guarantee different than FDIC insurance?
- Is term life insurance always the most economical to buy?
- How can you compare costs in different types of life insurance, such as term and whole life?

Life Insurance Company Quality

In the United States, major life insurance companies rarely go "belly up," and when they do their policyholders don't always lose a lot of money — although they may get somewhat bruised and lose oppor-tunities. In just about every decade, there has been at least one major fiasco involving a life insurance company. For example, in the 1980s, the most notorious failure was Baldwin-United, a former piano company that became one of the first leaders in selling fixed annuities. When Baldwin-United failed in 1986, the company had $3.9 billion of combined assets, and some fixed annuity holders had to wait years to get all their money back. In the 1990s, three high-profile failures occurred in the same year (1991) involving Mutual Benefit Life, Executive Life and Monarch Life.

If a life insurance company fails to meet its obligations, the "first line of defense" for insurance and annuity customers is the moral obligation of the industry itself to avoid a "black eye" of defaults. In many cases, including the four companies mentioned above, other insurance companies have stepped in to assume most or all obligations — although, in some cases, under modified terms. The second line of defense is state guaranty funds, into which insurance companies are required to pay premiums reserved for rescue operations. The strength and statutory limits of state guaranty funds vary greatly from state to state. But they do offer an important barrier of protection against a company's outright default to policyholders.

Of course, the customer's best defense against defaults is the financial strength and integrity of the company itself — and this is measured continuously by a group of "rating agencies." If you know how to assess the detailed data developed by these agencies (and available for free or at low cost), you will be in a position to choose quality companies with the help of a financial advisor.

Approximately 3,000 active life and health insurance companies are based in the U.S. and Canada — and three major ratings agencies provide coverage and ratings on many of them. They are Weiss Ratings (which rates about half the companies), A.M. Best (which rates about one-third), and Standard & Poor's (which rates about one-fourth). Two other analysts — Moody's and Fitch — rate just a handful of very large insurance companies. The top insurance ratings categories for Weiss, A.M. Best and Standard & Poor's (S&P) are shown in the table on the next page.

Top Insurance Company Ratings from Three Agencies

Rank	Weiss	A.M. Best	S&P
1.	A+	A++	AAA
2.	A	A+	AA+
3.	A-	A	AA
4.	B+	A-	AA-
5.	B	B++	A+
6.	B-	B+	A
7.	C+	B	A-
8.	C	B-	BBB+
9.	C-	C++	BBB
10.	D+	C+	BBB-

The bold-faced ratings above should be considered top-grade. They include the top five ratings for Weiss, the top two for Best and the top three for S&P. Approximately 220 companies in the U.S. and Canada (of 3,000 total) have earned these top-grade ratings from all three leading analysts. These are the companies that seniors should focus on primarily. If you want, you can drop down one more rank for each company —to include the top six for Weiss, the top three for Best and the top four for S&P. In that case, your universe of companies will expand to about 500.

I strongly urge seniors not to go lower than these ratings in selecting companies for their long-term mortality risk planning (life insurance) or longevity risk planning (annuities) needs. Why? You are choosing a company that must remain strong for the rest of your life —conceivably another 30 or more years .

The ratings are more accessible than many seniors think. Here are Internet links that you can access to obtain them:

- www.weissratings.com
- www.ambest.com/ratings/index.html
- www.standardandpoors.com/ratingsactions/ratingsinquiries.html

At the A.M. Best and S&P sites, ratings are available for free. Weiss charges a nominal fee per rating, but a qualified financial advisor might help you obtain current Weiss ratings for free. You should try to obtain all three ratings for the company you are considering. While Weiss is not as large or well known as A.M. Best or S&P, its ratings are considered by some authorities to be more "predictive" of future problems at insurance companies. The types of problems companies can encounter include having ratings downgraded by these agencies and being put on "watch lists" by state insurance commissioners, in addition to more serious problems such as potential defaults.

By selecting among products of companies that qualify for the highest ratings, you will be limiting your shopping to the "crème de la crème" of insurance companies in terms of financial quality. The table below shows the percentage of all U.S. and Canadian life-health companies that qualified for the top ratings categories in one recent year.

Rank	Weiss	A.M. Best	S&P
1.	0.3%	5.0%	4.0%
2.	0.8%	13.2%	8.7%
3.	1.5%	17.8%	8.5%
4.	5.2%		4.4%
5.	12.4%		
6.	10.9%		
Totals	**20.2%**	**36.0%**	**25.6%**

Shopping for Life Insurance Cost

Have you seen advertisements on TV that offer life insurance to seniors at unbelievably low cost — perhaps only a few dollars per month? Maybe you wonder what they **aren't** saying about deals that sound too good to be true.

Or, have you seen news reports claiming that the least expensive kind of life insurance is always term? If that's true, why are so many people paying higher premiums to own such popular "permanent" programs as whole life and universal life?

Confusion runs rampant in making meaningful comparisons of life insurance costs — but it shouldn't. You can use a tool that will allow you to compare the cost of just about any life insurance coverage on the market — apples to apples, dollars to dollars.

Understand the Differences

The first point to understand about life insurance costs is the difference between "affordable" and "economical." Term life insurance is almost always the most affordable for people on tight budgets because it requires the lowest cash outlays or "premiums," especially at younger ages. However, with term insurance, your money buys only a death benefit. In permanent types of insurance —s uch as whole life or universal life — part of your premium goes to build cash value. You then can use accumulated cash value to pay premiums in some cases, or you may borrow against it or withdraw it. Premium payments are always required in term insurance, but they are not always required in permanent programs — especially if cash value is large enough to pay premiums.

In every program, you pay a cost for "pure insurance coverage" to purchase a death benefit, and this is where economies can be compared. In term insurance, your premium equals the cost of coverage, but in permanent programs this is not the case, because of cash value build-up. For example, suppose you pay a premium of $1,000 a year for a given amount of annual term coverage and $2,000 a year for the same amount of universal life coverage. At the end of 10 years, you own nothing in the term program and your cash value in the universal life is worth $20,000. In which program is the cost of coverage more economical?

The life insurance industry has developed a tool to help you answer that question. Called "net surrender cost index," it is included by most companies on their "illustrations" of hypothetical policy benefits. This index assumes that you "surrender" a policy at the end of a predetermined period and take back any cash value, accumulated dividends or other benefits. It then calculates your net cost on a time-weighted basis to allow an apples-to-apples comparison of actual life insurance coverage costs over time. To apply this tool, just request illustrations on competing programs and compare the net surrender cost index over a period of years that matches your need for life insurance. (The 20-year index is often used as a benchmark for comparing costs on life insurance illustrations.)

Cost Isn't Everything

The net surrender cost index will help you compare dollars spent on coverage, but there are other features to consider, too. For example, one potentially valuable feature for seniors is the guaranteed coverage period. Some term insurance programs can't be continued beyond age 75 or 80, while many permanent programs can be extended to age 90 or beyond. Also important is the quality of professional service that assists you in reviewing and revising your program. Those cheap term programs advertised on TV are usually "do-it-yourself." On the other hand, many other life insurance programs offer the valuable continuing service of a professional advisor.

Before choosing a life insurance deal at rock-bottom prices, consider the advantages of asking a professional to help you compare your choices and costs, while coordinating your life insurance coverage with other financial needs. That's where you'll find the real economies over time.

Chapter 22

•••••••••••••

ILITs: How to Max
Your Estate Tax Advantages

I once had a senior client tell me: "Life isn't fair, Bob, because multi-millionaires get all the tax breaks."

I asked him what he was talking about specifically. He said: "You know, like the Rockefellers and Kennedys. The laws are written to let them pass money from one generation to the next with no taxes."

I had to tell him that he was confusing knowledge with privilege. There are no tax breaks written to benefit only people like the Rockefellers and Kennedys. It's just that families like those — that are both rich and smar t— know how to use all the tax breaks that exist. Many middle-income seniors could apply the very same breaks, if they just knew how.

In fact, you can pass virtually unlimited amounts of assets to the next generation without any income or estate tax consequences, by using a combination of life insurance and the somewhat obscure and very valuable technique known as an Irrevocable Life Insurance Trust (ILIT), as mentioned earlier.

At The Senior Financial Center, we've used this tool to work closer with our clients' estate planning attorneys and shelter literally millions of dollars from federal estate taxes, while bypassing probate and increasing the professional supervision of assets to reward multiple heirs. In this chapter, I'll describe how ILITs work.

How an ILIT Works

In concept, an ILIT is relatively simple. The person who sets up the trust (the grantor) is insured under a permanent life insurance contract (such as whole life or universal life) owned by an irrevocable trust. In such a trust, the grantor gives up ownership and control. Premiums on the life insurance typically are paid by the grantor through annual gifts. These gifts have no estate tax consequences if they are less than $11,000 per beneficiary per year and qualify as a "present interest." (More on this later.)

At the grantor's death, the life insurance pays a death benefit that is income tax-free. Because the grantor has given up rights of ownership, the life insurance proceeds generally are not included in the grantor's estate for estate tax purposes. Virtually all of the death benefit can pass to heirs without tax erosion. Also, the trust can continue to hold money after the grantor's death and manage it for the future benefit of heirs, using investment strategies that the grantor selects at trust creation. An ILIT can be especially useful in providing for the future care of minor children, and even children yet unborn, when it utilizes professional management after the grantor's death.

Technicalities Make ILITs Complex

It's the technicalities that make ILITs tricky and require professional expertise to plan. For example, the law requires that the life insurance be held in trust at least five years if the insurance benefit is to escape estate tax at the owner's death. This so-called "look-back provision" is designed to discourage ILIT creation in anticipation of death. Some professionals plan around this technicality by purchasing an additional term life insurance rider, enough to pay the estate tax in the first five years of the program.

Another technical necessity is to make sure that the life insurance is purchased and owned by the trust, even though the grantor is the insured person. Most professionals advise against having the grantor purchase the insurance and then transfer ownership to the trust. Instead, they recommend having the trust apply for and own the life insurance from the outset.

Yet another complex area involves the Crummey powers that must be written into the trust document, if the annual premiums are to avoid gift tax consequence. Using these powers, named after a landmark legal case, the life insurance premiums that the donor pays each year can qualify for the annual gift tax exclusion (currently $11,000 per person) if they are of a present interest. The Crummey court case held that premiums are of a present interest if beneficiaries have even a temporary right to withdraw them. In practice, beneficiaries who are granted Crummey powers rarely withdraw premiums, but they must be legally notified of this right periodically.

Trust Documents Must Be Customized

ILITs are not for everyone because they require the owner to have enough confidence and self-sufficiency to give up ownership and control of what may become a significant asset, the life insurance policy. Also, they aren't boilerplate trusts that can be set up with fill-in-the-blank forms. Each ILIT trust document should be custom designed, because the grantor must give up control to a third-party trustee — either a trusted individual or a professional trust company (also known as a corporate trustee). Specific instructions must be written in the document for the trustee to follow on such important matters as how life insurance proceeds will be managed after the grantor's death and whether the trustee can exercise discretion in managing assets or distributing them to heirs.

For example, if the trust is designed to benefit your four grandchildren, can the trustee pay out more money to those needing help with college expenses? Can the trustee make discretionary payments or arrangements to provide for a beneficiary with special needs, such as a learning-disabled child? As the grantor, you can be creative and specific in giving instructions during the trust design process, and you may have limited flexibility to influence the trustee later.

The Choice of Insurance

Another important issue is the type of insurance that will fund the program. When a married couple wants to leave a legacy, professionals may recommend a "survivorship policy" that pays a death benefit at the second death. When the goal is to shelter a pool of investment assets from taxes, regardless how large assets may grow, a universal life contract may make sense. In universal life, the rate credited to cash value each year will vary with current interest rates. So, it is possible to build more cash value when interest rates go higher.

ILITs can have advantages during the grantor's life, as well as after death. For example, the amounts paid as premiums (and future appreciation on these amounts) are removed from the grantor's current income tax picture and future estate.

If you are interested in setting up an ILIT, you probably will need at least two professional advisors to assist you. One is a trust attorney capable of drafting your document. Unless you already have a personal attorney competent in this area, it's best to seek a specialist who keeps up to date with ILIT regulations. The second advisor you may need will help you implement the trust and select solutions and vendors, including life insurance program and professional trust company. This advisor should specialize in helping seniors create integrated retirement and estate planning programs, as we do at The Senior Financial Center.

If you think an ILIT may make sense for your planning and estate wishes, now is the best time to talk to a professional. Remember the look-back rule, requiring that the trust be funded at least five years to have optimal estate tax consequences. It makes planning ahead critical. Also, think about how much better you will feel once you have a well conceived plan in place for the rest of your life, and beyond.

Chapter 23

••••••••••••••

Our "Wealth Enhancement Strategy"

Many seniors we have met believe (based on hard experience) that "there is no free lunch." No single financial strategy offers everything. There has to be a catch somewhere.

In most cases, that is absolutely true!

So, let's get specific about the goals you would like to achieve in retirement. Answering the six questions below may help.

1. Do you want to generate enough retirement income to support a quality lifestyle?

2. Do you want to receive guaranteed income that you can't outlive?

3. Do you want this income to be tax-advantaged?

4. Do you want to leave assets to your heirs in the most cost-effective, tax-efficient way possible — without having these assets pass through probate?

5. Do you have multiple heirs and wish to avoid friction or disputes among them?

6. Would you like to be totally free of IRS minimum distribution requirements on your IRA money for the rest of your life?

If you answered "yes" to most of these questions, you can address all of these goals in one strategy we have created for the benefit of our clients at The Senior Financial Center. We call it our Wealth Enhancement Strategy, and it can work for your retirement plan money (such as an IRA) or your regular savings.

To illustrate, let's use an example of a 70-year-old single woman whom we'll call Louise. Her average life expectancy is about another 18 years. She has financial assets of approximately $400,000, almost all of which are in bank CDs and savings deposits earning about 3%. So, the annual income produced by her savings is approximately $12,000. Along with her Social Security and a small pension from her deceased husband, she manages to maintain a modest lifestyle. If she had the means, she would like to fix up her house, buy a new car and travel more. She is very devoted to her children and grandchildren, and it's very important to her to leave them something when she goes. If she can keep her principal intact, then her estate might eventually divide $400,000 among them.

The First Step: Increase Current Income

The first step in this strategy is to select a guaranteed immediate annuity from a highly rated insurance company. By taking the "maximum payout" lifetime income option, Louise can increase her current income for as long as she lives. (At the annuitant's death, the immediate annuity payments stop and no principal remains.) Immediate annuity rates change often, but we'll assume that she decides to put all $400,000 into a contract that will pay her $2,700 per month for as long as she lives. About two-thirds of every payment will be tax-free; the other third will be taxable income.

In summary, the "max" single life annuity choice will pay Louise an income of approximately $32,400 per year before taxes. So, she has increased her income (compared to the bank CDs) by more than $20,000 per year.

The Second Step: Providing for Heirs

But what about her heirs? They will receive nothing from the "max" immediate annuity payout when she passes. To address this situation, Louise applies for a permanent life insurance contract with a $500,000 death benefit. Since she is in good health, she is able to obtain a "standard" rating and an annual premium of $10,070. (For my thoughts on health issues for seniors in obtaining affordable life insurance, see Chapter 21.)

Since this is a permanent life insurance contract, the premium is guaranteed to stay level for the rest of her life.

After paying the life insurance premium each year, Louise is still left with almost $10,000 more income annually than she had before. Also, she has increased the amount she will distribute to heirs by $100,000, because the insurance death benefit is that much more than her assets.

The Final Step: Setting Up a Trust

As the final step in this strategy, Louise sets up an ILIT to hold the life insurance contract. Here is what will happen when she passes:

- The $500,000 life insurance death benefit will be paid to the trust, bypassing probate. It will be received free of income taxes and also, provided she lives at least five years after setting up the trust, federal estate taxes. In our experience, a life insurance contract held in an ILIT is the most convenient, cost-efficient and tax-efficient way to leave money to heirs.

- Louise can name a professional as trustee of her ILIT and leave very specific instructions for the trustee to carry out at her death. For example, she could specify that amounts are to be paid to any of her grandchildren who need money for college. A trust usually allows for more specific instructions to benefit multiple heirs than either a life insurance beneficiary designation or a will. This helps to prevent friction and disputes among heirs.

IRA Assets Can Be Used

In this case, Louise used non-retirement plan money to implement the Wealth Enhancement Strategy. But when IRA assets are used, there is one additional benefit — namely, you never need to worry about IRS minimum distribution calculations again (on this money). When you choose a "qualified immediate annuity" payout over not greater than life expectancy, the IRS says that minimum distribution requirements are met automatically. Since heirs also must pay tax on IRA distributions, the tax advantages of leaving them life insurance can be even better when you execute this strategy with IRA money. (If IRA money is used for the strategy, annuity payments generally are 100% taxable. But so are any other types of IRA distributions.)

One common question we hear about the Wealth Enhancement Strategy is: "Suppose I need a lump sum of money, in addition to a monthly income?" The solution is to tailor the strategy to meet this need, perhaps by putting only part of your assets into the immediate annuity. Actually, an important benefit of this strategy is that it can be customized to each client of The Senior Financial Center.

When people tell you that no strategy can meet all retirement needs, don't automatically accept the advice. If your goals line up with the six questions posed at the beginning of this chapter, the Wealth Enhancement Strategy may make sense for at least part of your retirement assets.

Chapter 24

••••••••••••

Reverse Mortgages: Look Before You Leap

Once seniors have set up their retirement plans, they may find that their incomes about match spending needs, which means budgets are pretty tight. Where can you find extra cash to spend on the amenities of a golden retirement? Lately, a lot of seniors have been looking at reverse mortgages as a source of extra cash. In fact, they often ask us at The Senior Financial Center if we think reverse mortgages are a good idea for seniors.

I reply that it's a little bit like asking if a bank loan is a good idea. There are many ethical and honest lenders in your market, while others may fall short of that description. There are good loans available on attractive terms, for the right reasons, and bad loans that make no sense for anyone except the financial institution loaning money.

Usually, our clients ask us to help them decide whether reverse mortgages in general, or even a specific program, will work for them. In this chapter, I'll walk you through the counseling and evaluation process that we apply.

We begin with a six-question checklist to determine if you are a prime candidate for a reverse mortgage, and it is shown on the next page.

Reverse Mortgage Feasibility Checklist

	Reverse Mortgage Feasibility Checklist		
	Question	**Yes**	**No**
1.	Do you need more income or access to cash for specific reasons?		
2.	Do you own your primary residence "free and clear" of debt" (or with only a small remaining mortgage)?		
3.	Does the equity in this home represent half or more of your total net worth? (Do not count the present value of pensions or Social Security.)		
4.	Do you plan to live in this home for the rest of your life, or at least another five years?		
5.	Are you comfortable with the idea that your heirs might not inherit your home equity?		
6.	Are you interested in using part of the cash obtained from a reverse mortgage to make your estate plan more efficient?		

If you checked "yes" to four or more questions, then I would recommend proceeding to the next step, which involves increasing your knowledge about how reverse mortgages work.

An Exercise in Liquidity

Reverse mortgages are "liquidity producers." At best, they can turn a large and illiquid asset — the equity in your primary residence — into liquid cash. You can spend this cash to improve your lifestyle or you can apply it to other financial goals. Eventually, the liquid cash must be repaid. The repayment occurs:

- When you sell your home during your lifetime; or

- When the last surviving co-borrower dies and the home is sold. (If two spouses co-sign the reverse mortgage agreement, repayment occurs on the last death.)

When you take out a reverse mortgage and spend the cash, you are spending down your home equity.

The amount that is repaid from the proceeds of the home's sale includes the total of cash advanced plus interest and fees. At the time you enter the agreement, the lender must, by law, provide you with a "total loan cost analysis" or "total amount loan cost" (TALC) that discloses costs. It's smart to compare TALCs from two or more lending sources.

The reverse mortgage lender usually wants to take a "first mortgage" collateral position in your house, which means that you either must: 1) own the house free and clear when this mortgage is taken; or 2) use the reverse mortgage cash to pay down any existing mortgages on the same house. The reverse mortgage may only be written on a primary residence that you occupy.

How much cash can you obtain, and how is it made available? Each lender has guidelines for the cash advance ceiling, and they vary with the value of your home, local market conditions and your age. Older seniors can obtain more cash than younger seniors. The more valuable your home is, the greater the collateral value and the more cash you can obtain.

Because reverse mortgages can be complex transactions, with a number of fees attached, I urge seniors not to take them unless they really need more cash or income, and only then if they plan to stay in their home several more years. The great advantage of reverse mortgages, compared to other types of borrowing, is that they don't require regular repayment, which eats into your budget. This also can be a negative, because when you're not paying back debt regularly, it's easy to think of it as "free money."

Two Complex Features

Two features associated with reverse mortgages are difficult for seniors to understand, and one is a positive while the other is negative.

- **Positive** — Regardless what happens to your home value or local real estate market, you can't be required to pay back more money (if you sell your home) than it is worth. Reverse mortgages are considered "non-recourse financing." If home prices in your market ever do decline sharply, part of the risk is absorbed by the lender.

- **Negative** — The presence of a reverse mortgage does not affect the capital gains you will owe if you sell your home. In the worst case, it is possible to sell a home in which you have zero or little equity left but owe capital gains tax. This possibility is greatly reduced if you qualify for the Section 121 exclusion discussed in Chapter 31.

You can access cash under a reverse mortgage in several ways, including: 1) a lump-sum payment at the time the deal is closed; 2) a credit line that you can draw down as you wish; or 3) periodic advances, which allow you to budget an extra amount of income every month or quarter. You are not required to repay any amounts until the home is sold, but you may refinance the mortgage by paying off all amounts owed, if you wish. You must continue paying all normal expenses of your home, including property taxes, insurance and repairs.

Shopping Ideas

How should you shop for reverse mortgages? It's a good idea to start by asking lenders if they offer Home Equity Conversion Mortgages (HECMs). These are the only reverse mortgages on the market that are federally insured by the Federal Housing Administration (FHA). If a mortgage lender fails to meet obligations, the FHA will step in and fulfill payments to investors who have purchased these mortgages. HECMs generally allows senior homeowners to access the largest amount of cash at standard and affordable fees, and with all terms disclosed clearly. If HECMs are not available in your market, the best alternative may be reverse mortgage programs guaranteed by state or local governments.

The next shopping step might be to compare a reverse mortgage with the best home equity lines of credit available. There are two major differences between borrowing money under a reverse mortgage and a home equity line of credit:

- You don't have to repay any reverse mortgage interest until your home is sold, while home equity lines usually require current payments.

- Home equity lines of credit usually are simpler to arrange, require less paperwork and incur fewer costs. They also offer more flexibility in repaying loan principal.

If the cash need is temporary, a home equity line of credit usually should be chosen over a reverse mortgage. I think reverse mortgages work best for seniors who are in good health, plan to live in their own homes a long time and don't mind the idea that their home equity won't pass to heirs. Also, if you are "house rich and cash poor," reverse mortgages can help to achieve a better balance between liquid cash and home equity. If your retirement budget is stretched and half or more of your total net worth is tied up in home equity, reverse mortgages can be a viable solution for unlocking equity.

Home Equity and Your Heirs

What about the value of your home equity to your estate and heirs? Many seniors have this idea in the back of their minds: "I'll spend my money and enjoy life while I can. Then, when I'm gone, I'll leave the house to my kids and grandkids."

Is that a smart idea? It may not be, for several reasons.

- To get their inheritance, your heirs will have to put your home on the market in a real estate climate that may not be the most favorable. Everyone will know why they need to sell the home, and that could affect the price buyers will pay. Your heirs will have to decide on an asking price and choose a realtor to show the house. Then, they must agree on how to split up the selling costs and taxes.

- Under current law, your heirs will not owe a capital gain on a house inherited at death, since their basis will be "stepped-up" to market value at death. However, they may need to obtain a professional appraisal to determine home value at death.

- Each spouse's share of home equity is included in his/her taxable estate for federal estate tax purposes. Unlike cash or securities, houses are not assets that can easily be "gifted away" during your lifetime by using your annual gift tax exclusion (currently $11,000 per year).

- Even after your death, it could be emotionally difficult for multiple heirs to dispose of your home without conflict. For example, what if one of your children or grandchildren wants to keep your home "in the family" and live in it? What if your heirs can't agree on an asking price?

If you are considering leaving your home equity to heirs, an alternative solution that can make sense involves: 1) taking a reverse mortgage to free up cash; and 2) using part of the cash to pay life insurance premiums on a policy placed in an ILIT for the future benefit or your heirs. This strategy can help to simplify the logistical, emotional and tax issues involved in selling a house after death. If you must leave your home later in life due to poor health, it gives you more control in making important decisions, since your heirs won't be looking over your shoulder to protect their inheritance. Their inheritance will be securely held in a trust, which can divide benefits according to your wishes among multiple heirs.

When seniors tell me they are interested in reverse mortgages, I usually want to explore with them the reasons why they need more money and what they hope to accomplish with this money. If those reasons can make their retirement/estate plan even better, it's a good indication that a reverse mortgage can make sense.

Chapter 25

•••••••••••••

Investing for Retirement: A Question of Risk

After the big bear market of 2000–2002, I talked to many seniors who said something like: "I once thought stocks and mutual funds would be a big part of my retirement plan, and then they crashed. Now, I have a lot less money left to worry about in those investments. And I'm confused. What should I do? Get out of the market or stay in?"

Instead of trying to impart wisdom, I'd start by asking them a simple question: "What have you learned from your stock market experience?" Invariably, they would say that they know more about risk now than before losing so much money. I'd tell them that they went back to college, to the "University of Risk," and paid a steep tuition to learn the lessons that every investor should know before venturing into the stock market during retirement.

The main point in these conversations is simple: Learn from your own experience and the experience of other seniors. The stock market has always been a competitive (even cutthroat) place, where you should not go unless you feel informed and confident about all risks. The stock market mirrors and magnifies all the uncertainties that exist in the world. It changes your net worth every day and can definitely affect your feelings of happiness and security.

As a simple rule of thumb, we teach our clients at The Senior Financial Center the "Rule of 100." You subtract your current age from 100, and the remainder is the **maximum** percentage of your assets you should allocate to equities (stocks and stock mutual funds). For example, an 85-year-old person should commit no more than 15% of total investments to equities. There are often reasons why seniors should put less money in equities than this rule calls for. Rarely have we seen situations in which greater equity exposure is warranted.

Distorted Market Data

On top of all that, you should not believe all that you hear about the stock market, even from reputable financial institutions and advisors, because facts and figures often are manipulated and distorted. Since seniors tend to have the assets that stockbrokers want to capture, seniors are vulnerable to half-truths (and worse) about stocks, mutual funds and the market in general.

With that caveat in mind, let's consider in this chapter the question of whether you can tolerate the risks in the market at all, and if so, toward what retirement planning ends. In the chapters that follow, I'll discuss strategies for managing risk and selecting appropriate investments, assuming you do decide to participate.

Some Stock and Bond History

Let's begin with real facts about how U.S. stocks and bonds have performed during your adult lifetime. For a starting point, let's choose 1960 — when you may have been entering the workforce or starting a family. The tables below summarize how U.S. stocks and bonds have performed long-term over the period 1960–2003.

- For measuring U.S. stock market performance, we use the S&P 500 Index, a benchmark that measures 500 of the largest stocks in the United States market.
- For measuring U.S. bond market performance, we use the Moody's AAA Corporate Yield Average. This benchmark tells you how much yield you could earn each year on a "basket" of bonds issued by top-grade companies that qualify for the highest ratings. It is not technically a measure of bond total return performance, because it doesn't count price changes in bonds. However, when you hold bonds over long periods of time (such as those being measured), virtually all the total return is produced by yield.

Stock Returns and Bond Yields (1960–2003)

Year	S&P 500 Index Annual Returns	Moody's AAA Corporate Yield Avg.	Year	S&P 500 Index Annual Returns	Moody's AAA Corporate Yield Avg.
1960	0.5%	4.4%	1982	21.4%	13.8%
1961	26.8%	4.4%	1983	22.5%	12.0%
1962	-8.7%	4.3%	1984	6.3%	12.7%
1963	22.7%	4.3%	1985	32.2%	11.4%
1964	16.3%	4.4%	1986	18.5%	9.0%
1965	12.4%	4.5%	1987	5.2%	9.4%
1966	-10.1%	5.1%	1988	16.8%	9.7%
1967	23.9%	5.5%	1989	31.5%	9.3%
1968	11.0%	6.2%	1990	-3.2%	9.3%
1969	-8.4%	7.0%	1991	30.6%	8.8%
1970	4.0%	8.0%	1992	7.7%	8.1%
1971	14.3%	7.4%	1993	10.0%	7.2%
1972	19.0%	7.2%	1994	1.3%	8.0%
1973	-14.7%	7.4%	1995	37.4%	7.6%
1974	-26.5%	8.6%	1996	23.1%	7.4%
1975	37.2%	8.8%	1997	33.4%	7.3%
1976	23.8%	8.4%	1998	28.6%	6.5%
1977	-7.2%	8.0%	1999	21.1%	7.0%
1978	6.6%	8.7%	2000	-10.1%	7.6%
1979	18.4%	9.6%	2001	-13.0%	7.1%
1980	32.4%	11.9%	2002	-22.1%	6.5%
1981	-4.9%	14.2%	2003	28.7%	5.7%

1960-2003 (44 Years)	U.S. Stocks S&P 500 Index	U.S. Bonds Moody's AAA Yield
Average annualized performance over full period	10.4%	7.9%
Years of positive performance	33	44
Years of negative performance	11	0
Highest performance year	37.4% (1995)	14.2% (1981)
Lowest performance year	-26.5% (1974)	4.3% (1962 and 1963)
Highest 5-year cumulative	28.6% (1999)	12.9% (1984)
Lowest 5-year cumulative	-2.4% (1974)	4.3% (1964)

Interpreting Historic Data

If you had put your money into both stocks and bonds in 1960, and just left it there for the next 44 years, you would have earned 10.4% per year (on average) on stocks and 7.9% on bond yields. This indicates that stocks have beaten bonds over time by an average of 2.5% per year. Stock returns were positive in 75% of the years, while bond yields were positive in every year.

On an annual basis, the gap between performance highs and lows in stocks was huge: from a high of 37.4% to a low of -26.5%. It was much narrower in bonds: from 14.2% down to 4.3%.

I believe the most important statistic for seniors is the historic returns over five-year holding periods. You just don't know where you might be, or how you might feel about investments, beyond about five years. Even if you held stocks five years, your range of annual performance returns would have been huge — from 28.6% down to -2.4%.

So, here's the bottom line of the facts about investment markets during your adult lifetime. If you hold stocks over long periods, you could have expected to perform 2.5% better than bond yields, on average. Over any five-year period, stocks were a roulette spin compared to bonds. Losing 2.4% of your money per year may not sound catastrophic, but when you compound it over five straight years, it means your principal declines by about 13%. If inflation was increasing by 2% to 3% over the same period, you could easily lose 20% of your retirement purchasing power in just five years.

The Best Time to Buy Stocks and Bonds

Here's another way to look at the same historic data — by asking the question: When in your adult lifetime would have been the best time to invest in stocks or bonds? Here are my answers.

- **Stocks** — There is one primary factor that makes stocks increase in value over time, and that is the profits (earnings) that U.S. companies are making. As profits increase, so do stock prices and market performance. Therefore, the optimum time to invest in stocks is after a period in which profits increased significantly more than stock prices. You can pick the exact point in your lifetime when that opportunity was greatest — near the end of 1974. For nine years, stock prices had declined a bit on average, while profits grew. If there was ever a good time for seniors to invest in stocks, that was it (in hindsight).

- **Bonds** — The best time to invest in bonds is when interest rates (yields) are high. Not only can you lock in an attractive current income — you also gain protection against any price declines in your bonds. The lower rates go, the less current income bond investors enjoy and the more vulnerable they become to rate increases, which can cause bond prices and total returns to decline. The best time in your life to have invested in long-term bonds was in the early 1980s, when yields on top-rated corporate bonds were in double digits.

Conversely, the worst time to invest in stocks is when prices have outrun profits for a period of time. That certainly occurred in the bull market of 1995–1999. By 1999, the U.S. stock market had moved perilously high for all investors, especially seniors. Yet, did any investment broker or firm tell seniors the truth about stock market risk in 1999? Perhaps a few did. Of course, they were drowned out by the chorus of brokers shouting: "Buy! Hold! and Pray!"

Likewise, the worst time to invest in long-term bonds is when interest rates are relatively low, based on historic results. The low yield you can earn just isn't worth the potential price losses you could suffer, if rates go up.

The Future vs. the Past

What is the difference between being a pessimist and a realist? One answer is the ability to apply your experiences and common sense to form an outlook for the future. For example, you can't assume that you will be guaranteed excellent health as you grow older, even if you have experienced minimal health problems in the past. We know from experience and common sense that seniors are vulnerable to health risks.

Likewise, you shouldn't believe everything Wall Street firms tell you about the stock market — especially if it conflicts with what you have personally learned or feel to be true. For example, can we assume that investment markets will perform the same in the future as in the past? I think not — for four basic, common-sense reasons.

- **A mature economy and moderating economic growth** — The U.S. is a more mature economy than it was when you joined the workforce. In the 1950s and 60s, the U.S. had the highest rates of sustained economic growth in the world. Now, we can no longer claim that leadership as a country. In recent years, China and India (two countries representing one-fourth of the world's population) have doubled our rate of growth in Gross Domestic Product. The U.S. population isn't growing at the same rate that it did in the 1950s or 1960s, either. In fact, it's only because of immigration (mainly from Mexico and the Caribbean) that our population growth is expected to remain positive. Our economy has been helped recently by productivity gains driven by technology. It's becoming more apparent all the time that more tech-driven productivity equals fewer jobs. It would be very realistic to assume that corporate profits in the U.S. will grow in the future at a long-term rate approximately 1–2% below their historic averages. That would bring the long-term rates of returns you could expect on stocks down into the high single digits.

- **Volatility and uncertainty** — The stock market thrives during periods of geopolitical stability, such as occurred after the end of the Korean War in the early 1950s and after the fall of Communism in the mid-1990s. On the other hand, the market can be a volatile and vulnerable place when the world seems uncertain, in turmoil or dangerous. We don't know how long terrorism will remain a threat, when it will strike again with 9/11 force, or what the impact might be. We also don't know what will happen in the Middle East, in North Korea or among militant religious fundamentalists the world over. The market is one of the best barometers of such uncertainty. More uncertainty invariably leads to lower stock prices.

- **Inflation** — For more than a decade now, the news about inflation has been too good to be true. But how long can annual inflation rates averaging approximately 2% last? Contrary to Wall Street propaganda, times of rising inflation are not a good time to hold stocks. It's harder for companies to increase profits when wages and prices are rising, and the uncertainty sends many investors fleeing from stocks into cash. It would be realistic to assume that inflation might average 3% to 5% over the rest of your life — higher than over the last decade but in line with the long-term average over your whole lifetime.

- **The Fed** — Will you see double-digit bond yields again in your lifetime? It's not likely, because over the past quarter century the Federal Reserve has become a much more effective regulator of economic growth, inflation and interest rates. The Fed botched monetary policy in the late 1970s and early 1980s and learned from its mistakes. In recent years, it's been quicker to change rates to keep the economy on an even keel, and far more wary of excessive economic growth and high inflation. Bonds are not very attractive in an environment of low and gradually rising interest rates because whatever interest you earn is vulnerable to being wiped out by declines in prices, if interest rates trend up.

Shades of Gray

When I make points like the four just mentioned, I have been accused by a few seniors of being pessimistic, even unpatriotic. It doesn't bother me a bit. In helping seniors plan ahead, I don't think my role is to be Pollyanna. Your financial security and happiness in your golden years shouldn't depend on an overly optimistic forecast. So, while I'm not a seer or forecaster by any means, I do try to paint a picture of the economy that is realistically and conservatively gray (not black or white). That way, you'll be prepared if things get worse and can live even better if they improve.

Here's another reality about the future that is different than the past. When you were a young adult, there weren't many financial choices available other than bank accounts, stocks and bonds. If your grandparents built a nest-egg, they probably put it either in the bank (or bonds) or into the stock market. Now, you have far more choices for your nest-egg, including tax-deferred and immediate annuities, attractive cash value life insurance programs, a variety of government and mortgage-backed bonds, mutual funds and more.

In the chapters that follow, I'll give you my best thinking on a variety of investment solutions you may be considering, along with guidance on how to evaluate alternatives and make the best choices for your personal needs.

Chapter 26

••••••••••••••

The Truth About Being Well-Diversified

Until the year 2000, the mutual fund industry managed to perform a kind of magic on the opinion of the American investing public. If you bought a mutual fund — a professionally managed pool of "diversified" securities — most people believed that you could make a big part of stock market risk disappear. By owning small pieces of many stocks, instead of big pieces of a few, you would be protected against falling stock prices. Or so the thinking went.

Reality proved otherwise. From 2000 through the beginning of 2003, many "growth-oriented" stock mutual funds lost half or more of their value. It didn't help much that you were diversified among 100 or 200 different stocks, because they all went down — swept by the tide of a historically deep stock market decline.

Painfully, many seniors learned an important truth about risk the hard way: Some types of investment risk just can't be diversified away, regardless how much you try.

For example, you could own an S&P 500 index mutual fund that is well diversified among 500 large U.S. stocks. These 500 stocks are components of the index because they mirror the variety of the U.S. economy, including diverse regions and industries. By definition, the S&P 500 Index is well diversified in regard to "stock-specific" and "industry-specific" risks. Yet, if you held an S&P 500 Index fund through the bear market of 2000–2003, you would have lost 50% of your money from top to bottom.

Holding 500 large stocks still exposes you to the "systematic risk" of the U.S. stock market as a whole. Regardless how many different stocks or stock mutual funds you add, you won't reduce this risk — and in fact you may increase another type of risk, which is the potential to underperform the market average.

For example, suppose you own 20 different actively managed stock mutual funds. You pay a management fee of perhaps 1% per year (on average) to 20 different fund managers, each of whom works to beat the stock market average. Since these managers work separately, not in concert, they probably will produce a composite return (before fees) that is similar to the stock market average.

Since actively managed funds cost more in fees than index funds, investors who own 20 arbitrarily chosen stock mutual funds usually underperform the averages over time by approximately the amount of fees paid. In effect, they pay high fees to own the equivalent of a giant index fund.

The Value of Asset Allocation

The best way to reduce the "systematic risk" of stocks (or any other asset class) is to begin by deciding what part of your total nest-egg you can afford to invest (and expose to the risk of loss), given your personal risk tolerance. Then, for the portion you choose to invest and expose to risk, spread your money among several classes — such as stocks, bonds and real estate. This can be accomplished through a disciplined program of asset allocation, which sets guidelines for each asset class based on your personal return objectives and risk tolerance. The next step is to diversify effectively within each asset class.

The Role of Cash

Cash has a special purpose in any plan based on managing risk and achieving true diversification. Since cash tends to produce more predictable and stable performance than either stocks or bonds, it is useful for adjusting overall risk. Even in a terrible year for stocks or bonds (or both), a portfolio diversified partly in cash can emerge without major losses.

This not only helps to maintain momentum toward long-term financial goals. It also helps investors maintain confidence.

I urge clients to consider all of the following parts of their "cash" holdings:

- Bank accounts
- Fixed annuities
- Life insurance cash values
- Money market funds

Then, as a rule of thumb, I recommend committing to cash at least your age as a percentage of your total retirement nest-egg. For example, when you are 60, you should commit at least 60% of your assets to cash. When you are 70, the cash portion should increase to 70%. (Conversely, as we discussed in Chapter 25 under the "Rule of 100," you should allocate to equities, at most, 100 minus your age, as a percent of your nest-egg.)

Important Questions to Ask

Here are some basic questions to ask yourself as you diversify your assets:

- **What is my risk tolerance?** A financial advisor can help you answer this question by understanding your goals and investment experience. The further away in time your goals are, the higher your risk tolerance can be. Younger people have more time to recover from a setback than seniors. If you are a senior in good health, you might have a longer time horizon than a senior in lesser health. In general, our counselors at The Senior Financial Center believe we must be careful with the assets of seniors because most do not have the time to make money back again.

- **How well-diversified is my current portfolio?** A financial advisor can evaluate your current holdings and suggest sensible steps that may increase real diversification. For example, many people enter retirement holding a variety of managed portfolios, including mutual funds, IRAs, 401(k)s, variable annuities and variable life insurance. It is possible that these portfolios as a whole are over-concentrated in one or two industries or even a few stocks. In some cases, it can make sense to select different portfolios that reduce concentration and increase portfolio balance. In general, I'd recommend looking at your whole portfolio through fresh "retirement eyes" and reducing your risk level.

- **How wise is the investment today?** All investment strategies have their day. During the mid-1990s, it was fashionable to diversify portfolios by mixing U.S. and international stocks — especially stocks of companies located in Asia. Then Asian stocks went into retreat, with Japan's market falling to a 20-year low. The historical patterns that made Asian stocks good diversification tools a few years ago changed — and this type of situation happens all the time. Each investment should make sense on its own, as well as in an overall plan for portfolio diversification.

Mutual funds can be a good way to diversify, and there are other solutions that also offer access to different markets while helping you focus more on asset preservation. They include annuities, permanent life insurance (with cash value) and individually managed investment accounts that tailor risk to your own personal profile. A qualified financial advisor can help you evaluate the solutions available for pursuing diversification. Once your plan is in place, the advisor also can help you monitor performance and make necessary revisions.

Chapter 27

•••••••••••••

Look Behind the Numbers
of Mutual Fund Performance

If you are a mutual fund investor, it's hard to resist peeking at those performance reviews published every year that list the top-performing funds. Of course, you hope your fund will be among them. Or you may be seeking new investment ideas among funds that have turned in top performance.

At The Senior Financial Center, we regularly sponsor educational seminars for seniors — and we often are visited by seniors who claim to know vast amounts about mutual funds. Sometimes, they will prove their acumen by telling us how high their funds have ranked — such as saying "my fund earned a five-star rating" or "my fund ranked in the top performance quartile."

At that point, I like to quiz them a little by asking if they have looked "behind the numbers." Usually, their only reply is to look puzzled and ask what I'm talking about. I then explain that investments are more complex than restaurants or hotels, and the performance story can't always be told with "star rating systems." In many cases, the real story of a fund's track record is more intricate than the simple rate of return quoted in magazine performance surveys.

When you know the whole story behind fund performance, you are in the best position to answer important questions such as: 1) Should I be investing in mutual funds at all? 2) How did a given mutual fund achieve its performance? and 3) Does the fund's performance justify risk taken?

Remember that mutual funds aren't pieces of machinery. They don't run themselves. They hire professional managers who develop investment strategies and make specific buy-sell decisions. The performance data is, in effect, the manager's scorecard. However, the manager may be doing a good job even if the scorecard doesn't look great at first glance, and the opposite also can be true.

Three Critical Questions

To look behind the numbers, investors should ask three questions that an in-depth analysis of fund performance can answer:

• How active or passive was the manager's strategy?

• Did the manager's performance more than justify risk exposure?

• How did the manager perform against "peers?"

At The Senior Financial Center, we offer to help any senior who attends our workshop or becomes our client answer these questions, and more. We often do this by making available reports prepared by the analytical firm Morningstar. You can access a brief version of these reports online at www.morningstar.com. Most seniors find the full reports that we help them access and interpret to be more valuable than the data Morningstar offers for free on the Web.

Active vs. Passive

An index fund is considered totally passive. Its investment decisions are made by a formula to match the composition of a benchmark such as the S&P 500 Index. On the other extreme are highly active strategies in which managers pit their insights, wits and skills against the market. What most investors don't realize is that there is a spectrum of semi-active or semi-passive strategies in between these extremes. In today's competitive mutual fund industry, some fund groups specifically target how active or passive they want managers to be.

One somewhat obscure statistic will tell you how active or passive your fund has been over a recent period, and it goes by the name of R^2. Think of R^2 as a scale of percentages ranging from 0 to 100. A true index fund has an R^2 of 98–100, which means that 98–100% of the fund's performance is explained by movements in the market as a whole. Now, consider a fund with an R^2 of approximately 90. In this fund, only 10% of the fund's performance is explained by the manager's strategy or decisions. The other 90% tracks the market.

Does that make this fund almost an index fund? Not exactly. This fund is about halfway between active and passive on the spectrum, because the market as a whole exerts such a powerful influence on almost all investments. (That's why it's so hard to diversify away the market's "systematic risk.") A fund with highly active management would have an R^2 of perhaps 60–75.

Keep this point in mind about R^2 and active management. The higher the R^2, the more likely a fund is to have performance that is about average, compared to the market. Funds with lower R^2 are more likely to be either big winners or losers, compared to averages. In reviewing performance of any mutual funds, you should ask your financial advisor to look up their R^2 data through a source such as Morningstar.

Risk vs. Return

If you are evaluating mutual fund performance over decades, you can afford to focus mainly on returns, rather than risks. However, most performance reviews rank funds based on periods of a year or less. It's important to take risk into account in evaluating such short-term returns, because the fund that is hottest in an up market is a good candidate to be coldest when the market turns down. Again, there is one somewhat obscure statistic that tells whether your manager is producing returns that more than justify risks taken, and it is called "Alpha."

Alpha is a measure of the risk-adjusted return produced by a fund manager's acumen and strategy. In general, an Alpha of zero is considered average. A positive Alpha indicates returns that exceed risk levels, and a negative value indicates returns falling short. Alpha is an especially useful tool to use in evaluating highly active (low R^2) strategies. A fund manager who can consistently produce an Alpha of 1.5 or higher at an R^2 of 80 or lower is on a winning track in terms of generating risk-adjusted returns for investors. Sadly, you'll find very few such managers in today's mutual fund industry.

Performance vs. Peers

Before you decide whether your fund's manager is a hero or goat, check to see how performance has compared with "peers" — managers of other funds with similar objectives. Two analytical services, Morningstar and Lipper, divide mutual funds into categories and then rank managers based on either risk-adjusted (Morningstar) or raw (Lipper) returns. Morningstar uses a percentile system that places the top-ranked managers in the first quartile and the lowest in the 100th. Lipper uses a quartile system, in which the top 25% of managers are ranked in the first quartile and the lowest 25% in the fourth. The longer the manager's tenure at the fund and the longer the period evaluated, the more meaningful peer rankings are.

How can you check your fund's R^2, Alpha and peer group ranking? You can go online at www.morningstar.com and access a free "Quick-take" report on the fund by typing in its name or symbol. Or, you can ask a professional financial advisor to help you access and interpret this information. If you continue to hold mutual funds as you move through retirement, it's important to periodically review not only their performance but the overall risk they add to your planning. In many cases, I advise clients to discard higher-risk funds as they grow older, to guard against the possibility of sharp declines they won't live long enough to recover. (**Note:** If you attend one of the free senior workshops sponsored by The Senior Financial Center, we'll generate a more complete version of the Morningstar reports for funds that you hold, and help you understand them, as part of our complementary service.)

Chapter 28

••••••••••••••

The Value of After-Tax Returns

When you want to know how your investments have performed lately, the simple answer is not always the most accurate indicator of success. The simple answer is the overall rate of return you have earned. The true indicator of long-term success is your after-tax return — earnings you actually keep after paying tax obligations.

Focusing on after-tax returns can improve your investment program in at least three ways.

- It can make you more aware of opportunities to use tax-advantaged accounts, such as retirement plans and tax-deferred annuities.

- It can make you more aware of the risk you are taking compared to the returns you enjoy after taxes. In some cases, you may decide that Uncle Sam is receiving too much of your return, without bearing any of your risk.

- It can help you project whether you are saving enough money to meet important financial goals, such as having your money last as long as you do.

What Are After-Tax Returns?

Your after-tax return is the portion of investment earnings that you keep after paying current federal (and perhaps state and local) income tax on any interest, dividends or capital gains. During the big bull market of the late 1990s, many mutual fund investors became aware of after-tax returns, because a number of funds paid out high levels of capital gain distributions.

The Securities and Exchange Commission (SEC) studied how much of total mutual fund returns were lost to taxes during this period. In 1999 alone, the SEC found that mutual funds paid out $238 billion in capital gains and $159 billion in taxable dividends, resulting in $39 billion of taxes paid by shareholders. The SEC's report concluded: "It is estimated that, between 1994 and 1999, investors in diversified U.S. stock funds surrendered an average of 15 percent of their annual gains to taxes." Following this report, the SEC adopted regulations that require most mutual funds to report after-tax returns, using standard calculation methods.

To take a simple example, suppose you buy shares of a mutual fund for $1,000. One year later, your investment has appreciated in value to $1,100. Also, you receive in cash $50 of taxable dividends and a $75 capital gain distribution. (You may reinvest dividends and distributions into new shares if you wish, but doing so does not change the tax consequences.) You would have received a total of $125 in taxable dividends and distributions. The tax due would be subtracted from your total return, to yield your after-tax return.

Two things are important to understand about the SEC-required calculations of after-tax returns. First, they always assume the highest applicable federal tax rate — not your personal rate. The highest federal rates currently are 35% on ordinary income, and 15% on qualifying stock dividends and long-term capital gains. Second, the SEC requires two separate calculations of after-tax returns: One method measures taxes on dividends and distributions only, while the other assumes fund shares are sold after holding periods of 1, 5 and 10 years. In the calculations that assume shares are sold, any appreciation in share value (such as the $100 earned on price appreciation in the example above) is assumed to be taxed at the highest applicable federal rate, too. Therefore, the SEC-required calculations of after-tax mutual fund returns should be considered a "worst case" example by most investors. The truth is — most investors don't pay taxes at the highest federal rates, and most investors don't sell shares and realize price appreciation after arbitrary holding periods.

How the SEC Rules Help

Where the new SEC calculations do help investors is in expanding their awareness of tax-advantaged investments. In a Traditional or Roth IRA, for example, any mutual fund dividends, distributions or share appreciation is not currently taxed. That means all the earnings produced by shares held in the plan can continue to compound toward your retirement goals. 401(k) plans, tax-deferred annuities and permanent life insurance programs (with cash values) also allow tax-deferred build-up.

An alternative to mutual funds that has gained acceptance among the wealthiest investors is a "separately managed account," in which individual securities are held in the individual's name and supervised with full discretion by a professional money manager. These accounts are not required by law to distribute earnings, and they can be managed with sensitivity to the investor's tax situation and needs. In some cases, positions with tax losses can even be sold near the end of the year to offset capital gains. However, separately managed accounts typically require an investment minimum of $100,000 or more, and the manager's fees can be relatively high.

If you are in a high bracket, you should know that Morningstar's free online Quicktake reports include several tools to evaluate the tax-efficiency of your mutual funds. These include Morningstar's calculation of tax-adjusted returns, a tax efficiency ratio and potential capital gains exposure represented in the shares. To access these reports online, go to www.morningstar.com and type in the name or symbol of a fund. Or attend one of the Senior Financial Center workshops and we'll generate them for you.

Uncle Sam Reaps Rewards While Limiting Risk

Consciousness of after-tax returns can help investors avoid frivolous investment activity in which a big part of gains goes to Uncle Sam. For example, Internet day traders take high risks to make short-term trades, in which gains are often taxed at the highest rates. Suppose that a day trader is very successful in this activity over a period of time, earning a 25% return and paying combined federal and state income taxes at 45%. However, the after-tax return falls to just 16.25%, at which point the risk may exceed rewards actually going into the investor's pocket. If a short-term trader is wiped out by heavy losses, only $3,000 per year of net capital losses may be deducted against ordinary income. (The rest may be carried forward.)

Projecting Investment Growth

After-tax return is the most important number to keep in mind when projecting whether your savings can help to meet long-term goals. For example, suppose you inherit $50,000 and want to know what it could grow to over 20 years. You think it's possible to earn 7% per year in a taxable account. On an after-tax basis, that could be reduced to the 4–5% range. On the other hand, suppose you put the $50,000 into a fixed annuity that averages a 5% return per year tax-deferred. You could enjoy just as much after-tax return in the fixed annuity — without the high investment risk. Since tax rates do change at the whim of Congress and may also fluctuate with your income, it's hard to project the after-tax rates you can earn long term. But in a tax-advantaged account, you can set goals with greater precision and monitor progress more effectively.

A qualified financial professional can help you assess opportunities to earn after-tax rates of return that match your personal risk tolerance and help you pursue important long-term goals. Just remember to focus on what you keep after taxes, not all you earn.

Chapter 29

•••••••••••••

Bond Investing for Seniors

If you went into the bond departments of major brokerage houses and listened to the phone conversations, you would learn that seniors are the biggest market for bond investments. Other superlatives you could use to describe some seniors involved in these conversations include "most enthusiastic to buy"…"most knowledgeable"…and (sadly) "most gullible."

Many seniors are eager to buy bonds for one major reason: They need retirement income. When short-term interest rates are low and bank CDs don't pay enough interest to live on, bond sales soar. Some seniors have years of experience in the bond market and can shop wisely for yield, quality and maturity. Others have virtually no experience or knowledge. They are prey to sales tactics that pump out whatever bonds the sales department is being paid to push.

I think there are three sides to today's bond market for seniors:

- **The good** — The types of bonds and sales tactics that benefit seniors and can help them preserve capital and financial security.

- **The bad** — Even in cases when bonds can work well for seniors, they often are pushed by salespeople who don't understand seniors or their needs.

- **The ugly** — Sales tactics that prey on seniors, especially those who are inexperienced or gullible. I'll identify several bond sales tactics that are misleading or outright lies.

The Good

At The Senior Financial Center, we usually don't try to change financial relationships that are already working for our clients. One gentleman in his 70s, William, said he needed our help with his retirement and estate planning and also wanted to keep using his bond broker. When we asked why, William said: "I've known this broker for many years and he knows what I need. He doesn't call me unless he finds bonds that are what I'm looking for."

William is a wealthy New Yorker, and here's what he said he is looking for most of the time: New York municipal bonds that are either insured or rated AA or better, with maturities not longer than 10 years.

We could find no fault with William's opinion. In his tax bracket, New York municipal bonds produced more after-tax income than most fixed income alternatives. By focusing on the highest quality tier of investment-grade bonds, he emphasized preservation of capital, in addition to current income. By limiting maturities to the 10-year range, he bought bonds that he could afford to hold to maturity, so he wouldn't have to sell them at a loss if interest rates increased. Also, he wasn't investing in maturities beyond his life expectancy, and he was diversifying his portfolio among many bond issues.

In our experience, few seniors have all the benefits that William enjoys in the bond market — namely, a combination of experience, specific goals, selectivity and a strong bond broker relationship. So, if you must invest in bonds, focus on obtaining these attributes, using the ideas that follow.

Bond Quality

Learn the bond's current rating from at least two of the two largest ratings agencies, Moody's and S&P. The table on the next page shows their ratings. Focus on the highest tiers of "investment-grade bonds," those rated no lower than Aa2 by Moody's or AA by S&P.

A high-quality bond is one in which the issuer's promise to pay principal and interest is considered strong. The highest quality bonds,

Bond Quality Ratings

Moody's	S&P	Meaning
Investment-Grade Ratings		
AAA	AAA	Gilt edge, prime, maximum safety
Aa1	AA+	
Aa2	AA	Very high grade, high quality
A1	A+	
A2	A	Upper medium
A3	A-	
Baa	BBB+	
Baa2	BBB	Lower grade medium
Baa3	BBB-	
Baa3	BBB-	
Ratings Below Investment Grade		
Ba1	BB+	Low grade
Ba2	BB	Low grade, speculative

issued by the U.S. Treasury, are not rated. However, many corporate and municipal bonds are rated by the bond rating agencies. In general, a company having a strong credit rating pays a lower interest rate on its bonds because there is less risk to the investor that the company will default. In the municipal bond market especially, you will find many bond issues that are "insured." This means that an insurance company agrees to pay bond holders any payments that are due, should the bond issuer default. Insured bonds usually merit AAA ratings and are considered very high in quality.

Ratings below Baa3 (Moody's) or BBB- (S&P) are considered non-investment grade. Bonds with these ratings are called "high-yield bonds" or "junk bonds" because they must pay higher interest to compensate for their lack of quality. Most investors stay away from these bonds, and preservation-minded seniors should avoid them.

Maturity

A bond is like a loan made by investors (bond holders) to the issuer. Its maturity marks the point at which investors get back their remaining principal and the loan is effectively terminated. Most bonds continue to pay interest on outstanding principal through the maturity date. By holding a bond to maturity, you stand to receive a return equal to its par value, assuming the issuer does not default. The par value is a round number, such as $5,000 per bond. But the price you pay to buy the bond will be more or less than this amount.

- If you pay **more than par value**, you buy the bond at a **"premium."** You will get back at maturity somewhat less than you paid.

- If you pay **less than par value**, you buy at a **"discount."** You will get back at maturity somewhat more than you paid.

The problem arises when you are forced to sell a bond prior to maturity. In that case, the price you receive will be determined by bond market trading, not par value. If interest rates increase, you could get back less than you paid, regardless of whether you bought at a premium or a discount. How much less? It depends on the maturity of your bond. In general, the greater the maturity is, the more you stand to lose by selling prior to maturity.

The graph on the next page shows approximately how much bonds with various maturities would change in price, given a 1% increase in interest rates. It assumes bonds are priced at $1,000 before interest rates change. For example, the five-year maturity bond would decline from $1,000 to $960 in price. The investor who sells prior to maturity could lose $40 of principal value, on paper, for every $1,000 invested. But the 10-year maturity would decline from $1,000 to $934, and the loss would be greater — $66 for every $1,000. Longer maturities would decline in value even more.

Rates, Prices and Maturities

Assumes 1% increase in interest rates

$960 $934 $918 $908 $901 $897

| 5 | 10 | 15 | 20 | 25 | 30 |

Years to Maturity

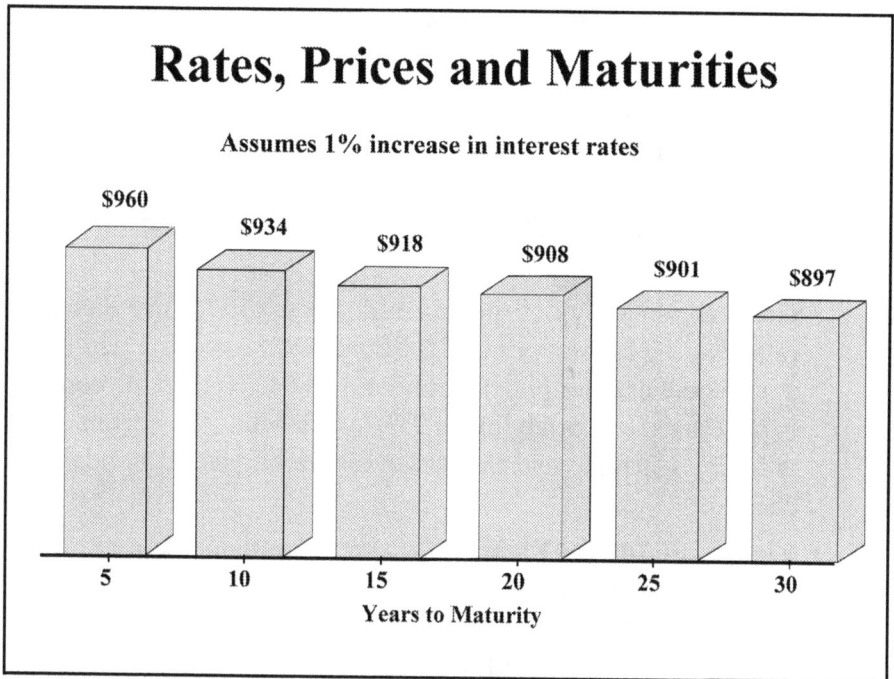

Approximately the opposite impact would occur if interest rates decline. Holdings would increase in value and could produce capital appreciation in addition to current income. This is why bonds can earn very attractive returns during periods when interest rates are falling.

Seniors can reduce their exposure to bond price declines by following two simple rules:

- Limit maturities to the lesser of 10 years or life expectancy.
- Buy bonds that you believe in enough to hold to maturity. (Bond mutual funds probably should be avoided because they have no fixed maturity. So, it is impossible to hold them to maturity and avoid price declines.)

Yield

If you have ever talked to a bond broker, you probably left the conversation dizzy with numbers — especially those regarding yield. Here's a sample of what you might have heard: "I can get you a 6.12% yield to maturity out to 2018 on a 5.98% coupon. That would give you 6.30% to the first call date in 2009." Unless you are an experienced investor, it sounds like Greek, so let's interpret.

- **Coupon yield** is the annual interest you will earn as a percentage of the bond's par value. If a bond with a $5,000 par value pays interest of $250 per year, it's coupon yield is 5.0%. Coupon yield is also called "nominal yield." It doesn't change over the life of the bond.

- **Current yield** divides the annual interest you receive ("coupon rate") by the current price of the bond, expressed as a percent of par value. For example, if a bond pays 5.0% coupon interest and is purchased at a price that is 95% of par value, its current yield is 5.26%. Current yield changes every trading day as bond prices change.

- **Yield to maturity (YTM)** is the average annual interest rate you can earn by holding the bond until it matures. It includes interest payments as well as the difference between your purchase price and par value. YTM will be above the coupon rate if you buy at a discount and below the coupon rate if you buy at a premium. Your YTM is locked in at the time of purchase.

- **Yield to call (YTC)** is like YTM, except that instead of figuring the yield you will earn by holding to maturity, it figures the yield to the first date at which the bond could be called by the issuer. A "call" means that principal is retired before the scheduled maturity.

- **Taxable Equivalent Yield (TEY)** is the most important yield calculation for tax-exempt municipal bonds. It tells you the yield you would need to earn in a taxable bond to equal the benefit of a municipal bond. To calculate TEY, you begin with the YTM that is currently available on a tax-exempt municipal issue. Divide this TEY by 1 minus your combined federal/local tax bracket. If you can find a taxable bond (e.g., corporate or U.S. government) paying YTM above the taxable equivalent yield, you probably should take it over the municipal bond. If not, the municipal may be the better deal. (The table on the next page can spare you the trouble of a TEY calculation.)

Taxable Equivalent Yield Table

Tax Bracket	Tax-Exempt Yield					
	4.0%	4.5%	5.0%	5.5%	6.0%	6.5%
	Taxable Equivalent Yield					
25%	5.33%	6.00%	6.67%	7.33%	8.00%	8.67%
26%	5.41%	6.08%	6.76%	7.43%	8.11%	8.78%
27%	5.48%	6.16%	6.85%	7.53%	8.22%	8.90%
28%	5.56%	6.25%	6.94%	7.64%	8.33%	9.03%
29%	5.63%	6.34%	7.04%	7.75%	8.45%	9.15%
30%	5.71%	6.43%	7.14%	7.86%	8.57%	9.29%
31%	5.80%	6.52%	7.25%	7.97%	8.70%	9.42%
32%	5.88%	6.62%	7.35%	8.09%	8.82%	9.56%
33%	5.97%	6.72%	7.46%	8.21%	8.96%	9.70%
34%	6.06%	6.82%	7.58%	8.33%	9.09%	9.85%
35%	6.15%	6.92%	7.69%	8.46%	9.23%	10.00%
36%	6.25%	7.03%	7.81%	8.59%	9.38%	10.16%
37%	6.35%	7.14%	7.94%	8.73%	9.52%	10.32%
38%	6.45%	7.26%	8.06%	8.87%	9.68%	10.48%
39%	6.56%	7.38%	8.20%	9.02%	9.84%	10.66%
40%	6.67%	7.50%	8.33%	9.17%	10.00%	10.83%
45%	7.27%	8.18%	9.09%	10.00%	10.91%	11.82%
50%	8.00%	9.00%	10.00%	11.00%	12.00%	13.00%

Note: Tax-exempt municipal bonds generally make the most sense for taxpayers who pay a combined federal/state income tax rate of 25% or above. Consult the federal tax brackets in the Appendix.

The Bad

The biggest mistake that seniors make in the bond market is to "chase yield." For example, they hear about a bond that is paying 7% interest at a time when CDs might be offering less than half that much. A bond broker tells them that the bond is "rated investment-grade," which increases confidence. But it's a bad bond for a senior to hold, because:

- It might have a maturity of 20 or more years — longer than some seniors can expect to live, on average. This exposes seniors to the risk of large price losses if interest rates rise. It also could expose heirs to difficult decisions. In my experience, the bonds that meet seniors' needs generally do not make a good fit with the needs of younger heirs. If your heirs inherit bonds selling at low prices, they may be torn about whether to sell and reposition the money into other investments or hold to maturity (and get par value).

- Just because a bond barely qualifies for an investment-grade rating today doesn't mean it will stay that way. Moody's and Standard & Poor's change their ratings all the time, and "ratings downgrades" are common. A bond currently rated in the lower rungs of investment-grade (e.g., Baa3 by Moody's and BBB- by S&P) could drop to "junk bond" status if the issuer's ability to repay declines. That would almost surely mean price declines on the bond, even if interest rates don't change.

- Some bonds are so thinly traded that it's not easy to sell them at a competitive price based on their yields. Holders who are desperate to sell these bonds become vulnerable to "lowball" bids, often made by market professionals who scavenge for deals among thinly traded bonds.

- The yields that sound too good to be true often are, for many complex reasons that aren't disclosed to investors. For example, you should normally expect to receive higher yields for longer maturity bonds, but if a bond has a call feature, principal could be returned to you much sooner than maturity (at the issuer's option). So, you may not receive the high yield for as long as you think.

The Ugly

Seniors should be especially wary of bond brokers who use deceptive or misleading tactics, especially when selling to the inexperienced and gullible. Here are some "red flags" to avoid:

- **"You can't lose principal"** — Don't believe any claim that your principal is "100% safe" or "your money absolutely will be returned." All corporate and municipal bonds involve various degrees of risk to principal, and that's why they are rated.

- **Unrated bonds** — A broker may tell you that a bond is high in quality, even though it has not yet been rated (perhaps due to an alleged technicality). Don't buy it. Unrated bonds have much higher default rates than rated bonds. Many of them would be rated "junk."

- **"Excellent collateral"** — Some brokers will talk your ear off about the collateral a company has pledged to honor the bonds. It's mainly doubletalk designed to confuse you. Think about it. Moody's and S&P hire seasoned analysts to evaluate bond collateral, and their opinions about collateral are built into their ratings. Why should you believe any collateral is better than these experts rate it, just because a self-interested broker says so?

- **"No commission"** — Brokers also may tell you there is no charge or commission to buy bonds from them. Well, you can bet they aren't working for charity. Often, you pay a hefty mark-up (over the dealer's price) to buy. In the past, these mark-ups haven't even been disclosed to investors. That is changing with more regulatory scrutiny.

- **"Only 100 bonds left"** — If you hear a bond broker tell you that a given issue is selling like hotcakes and "I only have 100 of those bonds left to sell you," just hang up the phone. Professional brokers don't engage in such tactics. They take the time to learn your financial needs and then scour the market to find bonds that fit them. Those bonds almost always are in plentiful supply somewhere. It's the broker's job to have plenty of choices on the shelf.

I hope this discussion of bonds will help you invest wisely. If you come to The Senior Financial Center holding bonds, or wishing to buy bonds, we will ask you why. What goals do you want to achieve with bonds? Why do you think bonds are appropriate for your situation?

Then, we'll tell you whether we believe bonds meet those needs better than other alternatives discussed in this book. If you wish to buy or hold bonds after we've been through this discussion together, we'll help you define the types of bonds that offer the best chance for success.

Chapter 30

•••••••••••••

Investment Planning Choices and Their Costs

In my experience, seniors are generally more frugal than today's younger generation, in part because seniors were born into tough times, the Great Depression of the 1930s followed by World War II. Seniors shop carefully for a variety of items, ranging from cars to groceries. When buying investment planning services, they have every intention of shopping just as wisely and getting their money's worth.

It's not as easy to shop for investment planning the same as you would a car, for example. You can't go into a showroom and see the base price and options itemized on a sticker in the window. You can't look up "going rate" prices in a Blue Book or check the *Consumer's Reports* ratings. You can't even compare prices offered by competitive dealers because it's hard to know exactly what you're comparing.

This hasn't happened by accident. The investment industry deliberately has made it difficult for investors to comparison shop or negotiate. Many investment costs and fees aren't clearly disclosed, and it isn't always apparent what services you are entitled to receive for your money.

Now, it's even more difficult than ever before — because many investment firms are switching from a "commission-based model" to a "fee-based model." In essence, this means they want you to keep paying them fees forever, as a percentage of the money you have invested. The going rate charged by most brokers has been about 2% to 3% of your assets each year. In this chapter, I'll help you become more knowledgeable about all the investment planning costs that you pay, especially these "forever fees."

A Story About Costs

Let me tell you about one senior who attended one of our seminars, Brian. Since Brian had worked most of his adult life as a CPA, he was smarter than most about money. And he was pleased to be paying his stockbroker a forever fee for investment planning, even after losing more than $100,000 in the bear market of 2000–2002. So, I asked Brian why he felt that way, and here's what he said: "When I pay my broker a 2% fee each year, instead of paying him commissions, he has no incentive to sell me anything. We sit on the same side of the table and we have the same motivation. My broker only earns more money on my account if it goes up in value, and he earns less if it goes down in value."

I said: "Wait a minute, Brian. You lost $100,000 with this broker in the bear market, so it's true that the broker is making $2,000 less in fees. Yet, you're still paying more than $5,000 per year to a broker who helped you lose $100,000. Does that make sense?" Brian paused a moment and then said he'd have to think about it.

I continued: "You say the broker doesn't have any incentive to sell you anything. Well, how many times during the bear market did the broker tell you to take money out of the stock market and put it in cash?" Brian said it never happened. I explained to Brian that these forever fee accounts generally don't charge much on your cash, so they have no incentive to take money out of the market. In fact, they really don't sit on your side of the table at all, especially in terms of preserving your assets in a down market.

I'm not saying forever fee accounts can't work in some cases. Just don't believe the baloney about these accounts making brokers more altruistic. Brokers still have a vested interest in selling you something —namely, keeping your money in the stock market, all the time, whether that's what you really need or not. Even if you lose big in the market, they keep earning forever fees on your assets.

Three Things You Pay For

Let's try to break through the deliberate confusion, by focusing on three things you pay for when you invest money.

Transactions

You pay to buy and sell investments, and this can be either a brokerage fee or a dealer mark-up. You can greatly reduce this cost with a buy-and-hold strategy. For example, if you buy $10,000 of a blue-chip stock, hold it 19 years and sell it, your transaction costs on this investment will probably be $50 or less per year. You can drive down these costs even more by using an Internet broker.

Investment Management

You pay a personal portfolio manager or mutual fund advisor a fee, as a percent of assets, to make buy and sell decisions and generate performance. If you need and want "active" investment management, be prepared to pay between about 1% and 2% per year. On a $100,000 investment, that's $1,000 to $2,000 per year. On the other hand, do you really need "active" management to achieve your objectives? You can buy passively managed index funds or exchange-traded funds for much less — about .25% to .50% per year — $250 to $500 on a $100,000 investment. If you buy and hold individual securities (e.g., stocks and bonds) there is no investment management cost.

Professional Service

Any good investment planning firm provides a variety of services that can be valuable to investors. These include: personal portfolio reviews, timely ideas, research, quotes, model portfolios, year-end tax reviews, and more.

So, here is my very best idea for managing your investment costs: Before you hire any broker or financial planner, decide how much you want to pay for these services and which services you will need. Then, tell the broker or planner what you expect to receive and what you are willing to pay.

Here is an example: "I have an investment portfolio worth $250,000 and my goal is asset preservation with conservative risk. I need a personal review once per year and timely ideas as they arise. I don't need research or quotes, because I get them on the Internet. I'm willing to pay your firm

$1,500 per year for these services, not counting transaction costs."

Here's the investment industry's dirty little secret. If all investors followed the simple wisdom of this approach, Wall Street (as we know it) would go broke. For decades, Wall Street firms made most of their revenues on commissions, by generating far more trades than investors ever wanted or needed. Now, these same firms are making money on forever fees, by offering services that many investors don't want or need and may never use.

Another part of this secret is the fact that even if you pay a forever fee—a percentage of investment assets annually — investment firms actually may be making additional "hidden fees" off your account that cost you even more money or lost opportunity.

Hidden Costs

One senior who came to see us, Toni, was paying a forever fee to a financial planning firm that specialized in "asset allocation programs." Here's how it worked: The firm filled out a two-page questionnaire about Toni's goals and then, 10 minutes later, suggested that she should pursue a "moderate" asset allocation model. This model determined that Toni should divide her money among seven different stock mutual funds, which she did. The firm charged her a forever fee of 2.5% per year for this program, which is called a "mutual fund wrap account." They told Toni it was a great deal because since she was paying 2.5% of her money per year, she wouldn't be charged any brokerage commission on the mutual funds.

Toni came to us disappointed because, over a period of several years, her "model portfolio" had trailed behind the S&P 500 Index return by about 5%. Here's what I told her: "You should expect that your mutual fund wrap account will lag the market benchmark by about 5% per year. When you combine seven unrelated stock mutual funds in one account, you actually get the equivalent of a big index fund. But that's before costs."

In addition to the 2.5% annual fee for the wrap account, Toni was paying an average of another 2% per year to the managers of her seven mutual funds. This was a hidden fee that her planner didn't disclose. In addition, all mutual funds have another type of hidden cost, their transaction fees to buy and sell securities. These fees typically knock another .5% per year off return, compared to an unmanaged index like the S&P 500 (which has no transaction costs). In total, Toni was paying about 5% per year to get the equivalent of a stock index fund that might have cost her just .25% per year. On a $100,000 portfolio, the difference would be $4,750 per year.

There is one cost-related question that very few investors ask their brokers or portfolio managers — namely, "How often do you trade?" The frequency of trading activity is expressed by "portfolio turnover," which is the average annual purchases (or sales) divided by assets. A portfolio with 200% turnover tends to buy or sell each dollar of investments twice each year. While this level of turnover is very high, it certainly is not uncommon. With each trade in a portfolio, there is a cost to the investor, often hidden.

Another type of cost technically is not hidden (because it is disclosed in a prospectus), but it might as well be. It is called a 12b-1 fee, or "trailer," and it is the equivalent of a forever fee attached to an investment product, such as a mutual fund. Whether or not you pay a commission to buy the product, the trailer keeps costing you money (usually between .25% and 1%) for as long as you hold the product. Most of the trailer is paid to the brokerage firm or broker involved, even if that broker is also paid a forever fee to manage your money.

In Summary

You can, and should, shop for investment planning services as wisely and frugally as you do for other products and services. By buying and holding investments long-term, you can save on transaction costs and reduce the hidden costs of "turnover." By using passively managed index funds, you can save greatly on portfolio management fees — especially if your primary goal is to preserve assets and seek conservative returns. Make sure you are getting the professional services that you really want. Pay only for those services you actually need and use.

Chapter 31

•••••••••••••

Eight Income Tax Planning
Ideas for Seniors

Seniors enjoy many financial benefits over younger folks. They may get a break on train fares or movie tickets. At age 65, they get relatively low-cost medical coverage under Medicare, and shortly afterward they qualify for full Social Security retirement benefits. However, in one area of their financial lives, taxes, seniors don't get many breaks. For example:

- Seniors continue to pay income tax on wages and earnings at the same rates as younger people. Since their dependents usually are gone, seniors can't claim as many personal exemptions or deductions on their tax returns.

- Working seniors continue to pay the same percentage of earnings into Social Security and Medicare as younger people do, even if they are receiving Social Security and Medicare benefits. Up to 85% of Social Security benefits also can be included in taxable income.

- Many seniors live on investment interest, pensions or retirement plan payouts that usually are taxed the same as ordinary income.

- Seniors are more likely than younger people to live alone and file taxes as single people. At some income levels, tax rates are higher for single filers than for joint filers.

At The Senior Financial Center, we do not work as tax attorneys or offer our clients detailed tax advice. We often work with our clients' CPAs to coordinate retirement and estate planning ideas with tax planning. In this chapter, I'll summarize eight ideas we have developed for saving clients income tax dollars.

Idea #1 — Home Mortgage Interest Deductions

The largest itemized deductions that many taxpayers claim are for home mortgage interest. When mortgage rates are low, many seniors take advantage of opportunities to refinance. The problem is that refinancing can result in extra taxes, because lower mortgage rates mean less interest is paid and deducted. But there is a strategy that can take advantage of lower rates available through refinancing without increasing taxes. That is to "refinance up" by borrowing more principal. For example, if you hold a mortgage with a $50,000 balance at 8% and can refinance at 6%, you might "refinance up" by borrowing $100,000. This will result in a monthly mortgage payment and interest deductions that remain about the same. But it will free up $50,000 in additional cash, which can be used to purchase tax-deferred fixed annuities. The strategy can produce a double tax benefit because it maintains mortgage interest deductions while producing tax-deferred interest in the annuity.

Idea #2 — Lower Rates on Dividends

A new tax law that took effect in 2003 reduced the federal income tax rate on qualifying dividends to 5% for taxpayers in the 15% and 10% federal brackets, and to 15% for taxpayers in all other brackets. This change has made stock dividends a more attractive way to earn retirement income, as long as you heed a few caveats.

- You must meet a holding period test to qualify for the low tax rate on dividends. You can't trade in and out of stocks just before their dividend payment dates.
- Not all stocks qualify for the lower rates. In general, the dividends qualify for the new lower rate if the company has already paid income tax on its earnings at the corporate level. Check with a company to make sure that its dividends qualify.
- In many stock mutual funds, a portion of income distributions will qualify for the new lower rate and another portion will not.

Most mutual funds report this information to their shareholders near year's end, but it does add to the complexity in evaluating mutual funds for retirement income purposes.

- Specific types of retirement income, such as dividends paid out by Real Estate Investment Trusts (REITs), **do not** qualify for the lower rates.

Even with the tax break on dividends, there are few high-quality stocks that will pay you a high enough dividend to compete (after tax) with yields on high-quality municipal bonds. However, a dividend-paying stock can make sense if its dividend rate (after tax) is attractive and its growth potential looks good. Pay special attention to stocks that have a track record for increasing dividends over time.

Idea #3 — Section 121 Exclusion

Prior to 1997, people age 55 or older enjoyed a special privilege of excluding up to $125,000 of capital gain from the sale of a primary residence once in their lifetimes. However, that privilege was greatly expanded after May 6, 1997, and now people of any age may exclude up to $250,000 each ($500,000 for a married couple) of home sale gain, at any age and as often as they sell homes (subject to restrictions).

There are two main restrictions on this tax break, which is called the Section 121 exclusion:

- To qualify, you must own and occupy the house as your principal residence for at least two years during the five-year period prior to the sale.

- You may not claim this exclusion more than once every two years.

For a married couple to exclude up to $500,000 on a sale, they must file a joint tax return, and both spouses must have used the property for two of the past five years.

This tax break makes home ownership one of the best investments a senior can hold, even for relatively short periods of time, provided you can make money when you sell the home. For example, the Jensons are a married couple who wanted to retire in their early 60s, right after their last child graduated from college. They also wanted to cash out their equity in the big four-bedroom suburban home where they raised their family and move into a simple, low-maintenance apartment. But they also had another attractive option, because they owned a vacation home near the beach. They had bought it for only approximately $130,000 many years before and now it was worth at least $400,000. If they just sold the vacation house, the gain of about $270,000 would be taxed as a long-term capital gain at 15%, because it was not their primary residence. But if they lived in that vacation house for just two years and then sold it within the next three, they could use the Section 121 exclusion again and cash out the $270,000 gain totally tax-free.

If you have the ability to fix up and sell old houses as a hobby, you can earn a nice tax-free income in retirement off Section 121. The only catch is that you have to live in the houses you fix up for at least two years.

Many seniors say that their own homes have been the best investments they have ever made. With Section 121, it becomes a tax-free investment, too, for most people.

Idea #4 — Living on Long-Term Capital Gains

Changes to the tax law made in 2003 created a wider gap between the top tax rates on ordinary income and long-term capital gains. For example, you could pay up to a 35% federal tax rate on CD interest. You would not pay more than a 15% rate on capital assets held for more than one year and sold at a gain. That "tax gap" of 20% is as wide as it has been in decades, and I believe it can hold opportunity for some seniors. (Note: On any income that is taxed at a federal rate of 15% or 10%, the long-term capital gains rate drops to 5%.)

If you have a hobby or passion that involves owning or collecting valuable assets — such as art, antiques, rare coins, or investment property — and you believe you can "buy low and sell high," there's rarely been a better time to do it. Just make sure that three conditions are met:

- You hold each asset more than one year to qualify for the favorable long-term capital gains rates.

- You keep accurate records of your holding periods and "cost basis" and report them on your 1040 Schedule D in the year of sale.

- You remain a passive collector or investor in these assets, not a dealer who runs a business in them. (Dealers do not qualify for long-term capital gains rates.) If you are in doubt about the differences between collectors and dealers, consult a professional tax advisor.

If you could "buy low and sell high" with any consistency, it's possible that a portion of the retirement income you need could be realized at very low federal tax rates (either 5% or 15%).

Idea #5 — Roth Conversions

One of the more challenging questions to consider is this: "Do you think that, on the whole, tax rates will increase or decline over your retirement?" It's true that major tax cuts enacted in 2001 and 2003 produced lower income tax rates for some seniors. But those rates are scheduled to "sunset" at various dates in the future, and the long-term tax picture is very cloudy indeed.

For perspective in answering the question, I've included the graph on the next page, which shows the per capital federal income tax collections for every man, woman and child in the U.S. over the past century, which is really the whole history of federal income taxes in our country. It only takes one glance at this graph to get the picture — namely, over the long-term, income taxes have always gone up!

What should you do if you think tax rates will increase during your lifetime? You might consider converting part or all of the money you hold in Traditional IRAs to Roth conversions. These conversions are allowed for single or joint filers with modified adjusted gross incomes of $100,000 or less. They allow you to pay taxes on the amount converted now, at current rates, and avoid required minimum distributions and income taxes later (at what may be higher rates). The mechanics of Roth IRAs, conversions and withdrawals are described in Chapter 9.

Individual Federal Income Tax Collections Per Capita, Per Year (1914-2002)

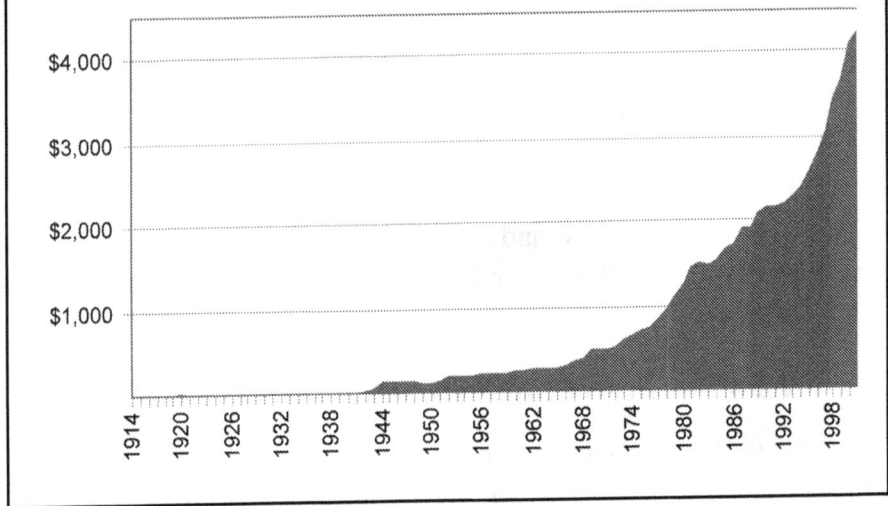

There are two points about Roth conversions that many people don't understand.

1. You can convert a portion of your Traditional IRA, if you wish, and you may make a series of conversions over several years. This can be an advantage because it keeps the converted amount (in a given year) from being so large as to push you into a higher bracket. Also, it allows you to look at your tax picture near the end of each year and decide whether a partial conversion makes sense.

2. Even if you aren't sure about the wisdom of Roth conversions, it can be useful to convert a small amount now. Seniors over age 59½ are allowed to take tax-free withdrawals from Roth IRAs starting five years after the accounts were established. So, by converting even a small amount now, you start your "five-year clock" ticking.

If you have large amounts in Traditional IRAs, in a way, a Roth conversion can be a kind of insurance for seniors against higher future tax rates. In essence, you pay your taxes now and enjoy your money (and any compound growth) tax-free later.

Idea #6 — New Perspective on Mutual Funds

Many investors ventured into mutual funds during the 1990s without really understanding how they work. For example, some investors in stock funds assumed that if they didn't take any money out of these funds or sell any shares, they wouldn't owe much in taxes. Wrong!

In 2000, the SEC became concerned about how much tax impact mutual fund investors were absorbing. After studying the situation in depth, the SEC concluded:

- For 1997 alone, U.S. investors participating in stock and bond mutual funds paid an estimated $34 billion in taxes on distributions.

- More than 2.5% of the average stock fund's total return is lost each year to taxes.

The SEC also observed that mutual funds vary greatly in the tax burden they distribute:

"The tax impact of mutual funds on investors can vary significantly from fund to fund. One recent study reported that the annual impact of taxes on the performance of stock funds varied from zero, for the most tax-efficient funds, to 5.6%, for the least tax-efficient."

Separately, the Investment Company Institute, a trade organization of mutual funds, reported that in 1999 and 2000 combined, U.S. mutual funds paid out total capital gain distributions totaling approximately $570 billion. These distributions were taxable even for long-term buy-and-hold investors who had never sold a share!

A diagram can help you to understand all of the tax impact mutual fund investors absorb, and it is shown on the next page.

How Mutual Fund Distributions Are Taxed

The mutual fund collects three types of earnings on its portfolio securities — stock dividends, bond or money market interest, and net gains on sales. The first two types are passed through to investors as an income distribution. The third type is passed through via capital gains distributions, which have a short-term portion and a long-term portion.

Portfolio Securities

Stock dividends

Bond or money market interest

Net gains on sales

Mutual Fund

Income Distribution

Short-term portion

Capital Gain Distribution

Long-term portion

Investor's Form 1040

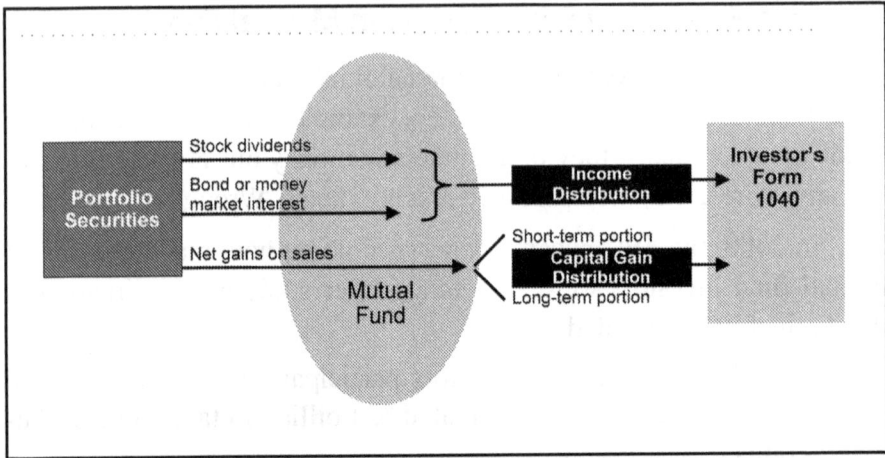

- An **income distribution** includes stock dividends and bond or money market interest payments received. Before 2003, income distributions were taxable as ordinary income. Beginning in 2003 and continuing through 2008, "qualifying stock dividends" collected by funds and passed through to investors receive the same favorable tax rate as long-term capital gains. Taxable interest distributed is taxed as ordinary income, at federal rates up to 35%. Tax-exempt municipal bond interest generally is not subject to tax.

- A **capital gain distribution** represents net gains on sales of mutual fund portfolio securities during the current year. It's important to understand that part of these gains may have been earned by the fund during prior years. Gains are "unrealized" until securities are sold, at which time they become "realized" and subject to inclusion in the capital gains distribution, typically made by most stock funds near the end of the year. The distribution often includes a long-term portion (representing portfolio gains on positions held more than one year) and a short-term portion (on positions held a year or less).

The bottom line is this: If you hold mutual funds outside of retirement plans, expect to pay some current tax, whether or not you receive any current income or sell any shares. If you own a stock fund that trades securities frequently, it may distribute a capital gain distribution in which a large portion is short-term gain. This is taxed the same as ordinary income (up to 35% federal), compared to the 15% maximum federal rate on long-term gains.

When the tax impact and fees are combined, many stock mutual funds become very poor investments for long-term buy-and-hold investors (outside retirement plans). For example, the analytical firm Lipper conducted a comprehensive study of mutual fund performance from 1992 –2002. It found:

- The "gross" average annualized return (ARR) of all mutual funds in Lipper's U.S. domestic equity category was 8.96% before fees, expenses and taxes. This was slightly below the S&P 500's 9.34% return over the same period, as expected because of mutual fund portfolio trading costs.

- However, the net ARR (after taxes and fees) of all U.S. domestic equity funds was just 5.19% over this period. The total of management fees and expenses, loads and taxes was 3.77% per year. (It assumed that investors bought and held the funds the full 10 years.)

- Federal tax claimed 2.27% of the investor's annualized return during this decade. Management fees and expenses claimed 1.30%, and sales loads .20%.

- Buy-and-hold mutual fund investors actually netted just 58% of the average gross return.

There were only two categories of mutual funds that proved to be relatively tax-efficient. They were tax-exempt municipal bond funds (as you might expect) and stock index funds. The index funds avoided large capital gains distributions because they seldom trade securities. If you must buy stock mutual funds on a long-term basis (in a taxable account), the data strongly suggests that tax-exempt municipal funds and index funds are your best bet when costs and taxes are considered.

Idea #7 — 529 Plans for Your Grandchildren

If you have grandchildren under the age of 17 whom you want to help with college expenses, you might take advantage of a tax-advantaged account called a "529 Plan" or a "Qualified Tuition Plan." These plans allow large contributions to be made on behalf of a beneficiary, using after-tax dollars. Earnings grow tax-deferred and distributions made for qualifying education expenses may be taken federally tax-free. As the account owner, you maintain control of the account and may even change beneficiaries, subject to restrictions. Investments vary by plan, but most 529 Plans offer choices among professionally managed portfolios with different risk levels.

Grandparents can set up a 529 Plan for each grandchild and put in fairly large amounts of money, if you desire. (Account limits vary by state.) These plans also can have estate planning advantages for the owner, and they don't severely impact a child's ability to qualify for financial aid. Below are some facts about these plans.

- These plans are now available in all 50 states and the District of Columbia. Many states offer only one state-sponsored 529 Plan, but you can participate in an out-of-state plan if you wish. Some states offer tax deductions on amounts you put into the plan (up to a limit), for state income tax purposes.

- For federal income tax purposes, distributions are not taxable if they are made for qualified college expenses, including tuition, fees, books, supplies and the care of special needs students.

- Withdrawals made for non-qualified expenses are fully taxable and also may be subject to penalties, at both the federal and state levels.

- Most plans give the account owner several investment choices, including age-based portfolios that automatically reduce risk as the child approaches college age.

- Fees are negotiated with financial vendors by each state, and they usually are very competitive and reasonable.

- A useful Web site for learning more about 529 Plans is www.savingforcollege.com

Idea #8 — Give Grandchildren Appreciated Property

Some seniors whom I've met have two needs that fit together beautifully:

1. They want to lighten their exposure to the stock market and reduce investment risk.

2. They want to help their grandchildren go to college, pay for a wedding or buy a house.

If you own stocks, bonds or mutual funds that are worth more than you paid for them, and you are in a fairly high tax bracket, don't sell them! Consider giving these "appreciated assets" to a child or grandchild. You can give away up to $11,000 per person per year without federal gift tax consequences.

If you are making gifts of appreciated assets to a grandchild, you might want to wait until the child is age 14 or older. Since children of this age aren't subject to "kiddie tax" rules, most pay tax in 10% or 15% federal brackets, which allows them to pay tax on long-term gains at just a 5% rate, under current law. (On a gift of appreciated assets, you pay no income tax and the child receives your cost basis and holding period.) Be aware that large gifts in one year could push the child beyond the 15% bracket.

Chapter 32

•••••••••••••

How to Select Professional Planning Help

Once you've decided to "get serious" about retirement and estate planning, one of your first steps may be to seek out professional help. Choosing a financial planning advisor and/or firm is one of the most important decisions you can make, and it also can be one of the most confusing.

After reading my ideas in this book, I hope that you will consider evaluating our firm, The Senior Financial Center, for the professional help that you need. Whatever you decide, my job here wouldn't be complete without offering my best ideas on how to choose a planning advisor or firm.

What is a smart process for evaluating financial planning firms and their service? What questions should you ask in evaluating professionals? What should you pay an advisor, and how can you determine if you're getting what you pay for?

Let's answer those questions with seven common-sense ideas.

1. **Focus on people** — As a senior, you don't want to go through the process of selecting an advisor more than once. You probably want a relationship that will continue for years and help you achieve financial security for the rest of your life. In my experience, this kind of relationship usually is built on a personal level. That's why it's best to set aside the advertising hype of big financial institutions and focus instead on the integrity, style, values and work habits of the people with whom you will work. Attending financial seminars or workshops is a great way to compare financial professionals, because

it allows you to evaluate personal styles before you make a commitment. It's why we've built our "get acquainted" process with new clients, in large part, on free workshops. I also recommend obtaining recommendations from people you know and trust, ideally those who already are clients of the same advisor.

2. **Be deliberate** — Some of the best advisor relationships are built gradually, so don't feel pressured to make big commitments fast. Tell the advisor what you want to accomplish, and don't let yourself be pushed into processes or products that aren't your priorities. You don't have to address all your financial goals in one or two meetings. Take the time to evaluate your options, and **don't procrastinate**. When you're a senior, every day counts!

3. **Listen** — In your first or second interview, most advisors will tell you how they work and what they do best. Sit back and listen carefully. Try to identify the advisor's strengths and decide whether these match your needs.

4. **Expect to be educated** — Ask professionals how financial concepts work, and then evaluate how much clarity and care they put into the answers. The best financial advisors are good communicators and educators. They don't mind teaching clients and they don't feel threatened by clients who ask questions. When advisors brush off questions with flip answers, it can be a sign that they want to push clients into specific products that may not be appropriate. Good advisors don't bully clients with their superior financial knowledge. They share it.

5. **Discuss fees** — In today's financial profession, advisors are paid in many ways. Some payments are made through commissions while others involve hourly fees or fees based on assets invested. Any method can work, provided you understand and are comfortable with it.

6. **Evaluate process** — At some point early in your relationship, the advisor probably will make a specific recommendation to

you, which can involve buying an investment or insurance product, participating in a planning analysis or opening a brokerage account. Before accepting or rejecting the recommendation, ask yourself a basic "process question" first — namely, has the advisor learned enough about you and your needs to make an appropriate recommendation at that point? If a recommendation comes too fast, perhaps after casual conversation, it's a good sign that the advisor is focusing on his/her needs more than yours.

7. **Remember your advisor's role** — Your financial advisor isn't your parent, buddy or psychiatrist. An advisor will prove most valuable when he/she listens to your needs, makes clear recommendations, keeps you focused on planning processes, helps you avoid mistakes or unwarranted risk, and always tells you the truth. When financial advisors exaggerate their skills or promise huge investment success at low risk, it's a big red flag.

Top financial advisors are busy people. Although they can't afford to spend hours a day on small talk or client "hand-holding," whenever you have a serious need or question, they will take the time to address it. Even if you don't have as much money as other clients, they'll recognize that your financial goals are just as important. They won't make investing or planning difficult for you. At every opportunity, they will try to simplify your life without glossing over difficult decisions or unpleasant results. Always, a good advisor will remind you that you are in charge of achieving your own goals, and you can do that best when you have the benefit of accurate information, objective analysis and clear recommendations.

In short, the best advisor will stay with you for the rest of your life and always build your confidence, while taking your personal financial security and happiness to heart.

Chapter 33

•••••••••••••

In Conclusion: What Makes a Senior Winner?

I've been working as a financial professional in the senior market long enough to have seen important patterns that identify people who are living to the utmost regardless how healthy they are or how long they may live.

I like to think of these patterns as a kind of profile that makes a "Senior Winner." Let me emphasize that Senior Winners don't need to have piles of money, drive fancy cars, or take exotic vacations. They can live in nursing homes or find the greatest pleasure working in their own gardens at home.

After careful thought, I've concluded that being a Senior Winner is mainly a state of mind, of which financial security is one important part. The other important parts are Activity, Involvement and Optimism.

Let me describe each quality briefly and then explain the role that financial security contributes to the profile.

- **Activity** — Senior Winners don't slow down much at "retirement." In fact, it can be hard to identify exactly when some of them retire, because they stay on the go and transition from work-related activities to personal enjoyment activities so well. When I meet with clients and ask them, "What's happening in your life?" Senior Winners always have a lot to talk about. Many of them keep learning new skills or languages and seek new experiences. Regular exercise — such as walking, yoga, tennis or golf — is a part of their lives.

- **Involvement** — Most Senior Winners stay connected to families, friends, organizations and events. Their calendars are not empty.

They keep meeting new people and forming new relationships. They care about and for other people, and they take the time and effort to remember birthdays or visit friends in need.

- **Optimism** — Senior winners can look back at all the accomplishments of their lifetimes with pride. They have learned from their mistakes and then put those disappointments in the past. They believe in the resourceful and resilient nature of the human species, and think that even the most complex problems — like the financial troubles of the Social Security system or the Middle East conflict — can be solved eventually. They are glad their grandchildren will not endure all the hardships they did growing up. They also believe every person can benefit from the experience of rising above adversities. They know that adversity has made them stronger and able to enjoy the best times of their lives—which is right now!

In short, Senior Winners live life to the fullest and they live in the moment. They do not dwell on the past, or worry about the future, because there is so much they want to do **today**.

Where Financial Security Fits In

Most seniors whom I've met have, at some point in their lives, made serious financial mistakes. So, here is how I define financial security to them: Real financial security means being confident you won't make the same mistakes again.

You see, so many people keep making **the same** basic mistakes with their money, and they aren't a secret. Here they are:

1. **Believing imaginary promises rather than reality.** The reality is that investment markets don't always go up. History doesn't always repeat itself. It's better to be safe with your money, especially as you grow older, than sorry.

2. **Buying into trends and fads instead of quality.** Wall Street isn't very different than the Paris fashion scene. If they don't keep rolling out hot new ideas, many people will lose interest and stop buying. Of course, you don't have to buy into financial fashions. Stick to high-quality ideas and institutions that offer

guarantees and the financial strength to back them.

3. **Accepting half-truths (when you know there's more to know).** Some bond investors want to believe the salesman's claim that "your money is safe," even if they have doubts. So, they don't bother to ask whether they will lose principal if interest rates rise and they must sell before maturity. Likewise, mutual fund investors want to believe that diversification reduces stock market risk, even if they have doubts. Trust your doubts!

4. **Paying too much for financial services you don't need.** You know how much you pay for services of other professionals, such as doctors and dentists. You should know what you are paying for financial help and you should not have to pay for services you don't need. Forever fees based on your assets can be very expensive over time.

5. **Paying more taxes than you must.** The IRS does not give "senior discounts." You can live better in retirement by taking advantage of tax-saving ideas and strategies. You also can avoid burdensome estate taxes on your heirs.

6. **Failing to plan for uncertainties.** For seniors, health is perhaps the greatest uncertainty. You can reduce your vulnerability to health costs by making smart decisions involving Medicare Supplement Insurance ("Medigap") and LTCI.

7. **Letting your money be lazy.** You worked hard to earn money for decades. Now, your money should work just as hard for you. Money that sits in CDs earning 2% to 3% taxable interest is losing purchasing power to inflation every year.

8. **Procrastinating.** Ultimately, you must take responsibility for making financial decisions. Seniors are different than younger people in two important ways: 1) Many seniors have a fixed amount of money to apply to their goals; and 2) They probably have fewer years left to apply it. To make the most of the money and time you have, make every day count. Don't procrastinate!

Seniors are like younger people in another way — you only have so much space in your mind for ideas. Senior Winners allocate most of their "mental space" for activities, relationships, travel plans, recreation and exercise. To do that, they must clear their minds of worries over past mistakes and fears about future risks and uncertainties.

As a financial counselor to seniors, I see my role as helping you "clean out your mental attic" and get rid of all those negative, nagging ideas that can clutter up your thinking and planning. In a few weeks of getting acquainted, identifying your objectives and making important decisions, you will feel a lot more free of spirit, as if we are opening windows in a dusty attic to let in fresh air and sunshine. Ultimately, I think it's that feeling of freedom, clarity and power that makes ordinary people into Senior Winners.

How can we start this process? However you prefer. But I strongly suggest that you attend one of our Senior Workshops (if you haven't done so already). At The Senior Financial Center, these workshops are always free of charge, and we usually throw in refreshments or dinner. It's a great way to reinforce the ideas presented in this book while getting personally acquainted. For anyone who attends our workshops, we offer a personal counseling session with a financial professional, also free of charge. Why? We want you to feel totally comfortable with our planning process and people before you decide to hire us.

The Power of Senior Moments

In closing, let me leave you with one final thought about a phrase that, unfortunately, has become a fixture of our language — "senior moment." (Since this term has developed something of a negative connotation, we prefer "intellectual overload.")

A senior moment has come to mean an episode of forgetfulness, and perhaps some mental confusion or inability to recall or act. Of course, our bodies and minds do change with age, and not all changes diminish ability. Even so, the stereotype of senior moments is real, and it even affects the attitudes that some financial companies have in marketing to seniors. In some cases, companies "dumb down" the facts they give seniors or talk down to them in ways that can be manipulative.

I hope you don't feel that the tone or substance of this book is "dumbed down," because it's exactly the way we communicate with our clients at The Senior Financial Center. We also have a unique view of the term "senior moment."

If you look up the word "moment" in the dictionary, you will see it has two meanings. The first is "a brief period of time." The second is "an expression of power or force," as in the word "momentum."

We define senior moments as feelings of clarity and power, in which you make decisions and take actions that keep you active, involved and optimistic. We believe that your life experience and achievements give you greater ability to achieve these feelings than when you were a younger person. Our role is to guide and assist you at important moments, when you make the plans and decisions that will move your life forward while maintaining its energy.

Here's to you...and your senior moments. (Or, if you prefer, your intellectual overloads!)

Appendix

•••••••••••••

How Long Will Your Money Last?

		Assume that you withdraw interest and principal at these rates.						
		6%	7%	8%	9%	10%	11%	12%
		Your principal will last this many years until it is exhausted.						
Assume	5%	36	25	20	16	14	12	11
your	6%		33	23	18	15	13	11
money								
earns this	7%			30	22	17	14	12
average	8%				28	20	16	14
rate.	9%					26	20	16
	10%						25	18
	11%							23

How Much Income Can You Receive?

The table below can be used to estimate the level of annual income a sum of money would produce (per $100,000) assuming that it earns the return shown and principal is exhausted at the end of the number of years shown. It is useful in evaluating immediate annuity payout amounts based on either lifetime or PC income.

		Assume you will receive an income over this number of years.				
		10	15	20	25	30
		You could receive this annual income from interest and principal (per $100,000).				
Assume	5%	$12,950	$9,634	$8,024	$7,095	$6,505
your	6%	$13,587	$10,296	$8,718	$7,823	$7,265
money	7%	$14,238	$10,979	$9,439	$8,581	$8,059
earns	8%	$14,903	$11,683	$10,185	$9,368	$8,883
this	9%	$15,582	$12,406	$10,955	$10,181	$9,734
average	10%	$16,275	$13,147	$11,746	$11,017	$10,608
rate.	11%	$16,980	$13,907	$12,558	$11,874	$11,502

The Four Most Important Lines of Your Tax Return

1040 Line	What it shows	Planning consequences
8a	Taxable interest	If you don't need this much current income, why pay tax on it?
8b	Tax-exempt interest	Be careful! Tax-exempt interest can increase the amount of your Social Security that is taxed.
9	Dividend income	Some dividends qualify for a low tax rate, but not all do.
20b	Social Security benefits	Depending on your income, 0%, 50% or 85% of your Social Security benefits can be taxable.

How To Reach Us

If you would like more information about *Financial Success for Seniors,* or other financial products and services, please visit us on the Web at:

www.seniorfinancialcenter.com

There you will find information on:

- Upcoming "Asset Protection for Those 60 and Better" Workshops
- How to subscribe to our free Senior Newsletter
- How to hire Bob Sagar to speak at your next event
- How to schedule a free personal consultation
- Information on our specialty booklets for seniors
- How to schedule an "Income Tax Return Review"
- For financial professionals: How to become part of The Senior Financial Center Network
- Audio tapes
- Videos
- How to arrange to have an "Asset Protection for Those 60 and Better" workshop hosted at your organization or company

You may also reach us by telephone and/or email at:

- Phone: 1-800-618-1825
- Email: Bob@seniorfinancialcenter.com

I hope this book has touched you in many ways. If it has, I'd love to hear from you. It will mean a great deal to me as well as everyone at The Senior Financial Center. Please understand in advance that I do read all emails and correspondence. However, I cannot answer personal financial questions or recommend other financial advisors.

www.ingramcontent.com/pod-product-compliance
Lightning Source LLC
Chambersburg PA
CBHW070522200326
41519CB00013B/2897